Collaborating with Community-Based Organizations
Through Consultation and Technical Assistance

Collaborating with Community-Based Organizations Through Consultation and Technical Assistance

■ ■ ■

Edited by

Patricia Stone Motes and Peg McCartt Hess

Columbia University Press   New York

Columbia University Press
Publishers Since 1893
New York   Chichester, West Sussex
Copyright © 2007 Columbia University Press
All rights reserved

Library of Congress Cataloging-in-Publication Data

Collaborating with community-based organizations through consultation and
technical assistance / edited by Patricia Stone Motes and Peg McCartt Hess.
    p. cm.
Includes blibliographical references and index.
ISBN 0–231–12872–X (cloth : alk. paper) — ISBN 0–231–50285–0 (e-book)
1. Community-based family service. 2. Family services. 3. Community organization.
4. Family social work. 5. Community development.
    I. Motes, Patricia Stone. II. Hess, Peg McCartt.

HV697.C63   2006
. 362.82'57—dc22   2006017593

∞

Columbia University Press books are printed on
permanent and durable acid-free paper.

This book is printed on paper with recycled content.

Printed in the United States of America

c 10 9 8 7 6 5 4 3 2 1

Contents

Figures

Tables

Acknowledgments

We are indebted to a number of colleagues who have invested deeply in this collaborative effort. Arlene Bowers Andrews, former director of the Institute for Families in Society, urged the institute's faculty to conceptualize and write about our collaborations with numerous community-based organizations that serve children and families. Without her vision and her confidence in our work and in us, this volume would not have been undertaken.

As coeditors and contributors, our process in developing this volume was somewhat unusual. Beginning in 2001, we met together regularly to reflect upon and conceptualize our professional work as consultants. As a group, we developed the book's focus and organization and subsequently collaboratively reviewed and discussed chapter drafts. The willingness of the contributors to engage in this time-consuming process greatly enhanced both the theoretical and practical basis of the book and its readability. We are indebted to all of our colleagues at the Institute for Families in Society who contributed in both large and small ways to the conceptualization of this book.

Throughout this volume, vignettes and case examples from our practice illustrate the text. We are grateful to the organizations with which our consultation, technical assistance, and collaborative practice occurred for giving permission for these illustrations to be included.

We also consistently received excellent editorial and technical support from Renée Gibson, public information director at IFS. As a member of our collaborative team, Renée brought her multifaceted competencies to bear on the manuscript and assisted in final editing and formatting as well as the design of the volume's graphic illustrations.

At critical decision points throughout the process, we also received invaluable guidance from the social work editorial staff of Columbia University Press: the late John Michel, Shelly Reinhardt, and, most recently, Lauren Dockett. We also recognize the contributions of the anonymous peer reviewers who provided insightful feedback and wise suggestions, thereby improving the final product.

And finally, we are deeply grateful to the countless professional practitioners and community professionals, service consumers, and the staff of funding organizations whose collaborations with us have shaped and informed our knowledge, our skills, and our understanding of what is needed to support and strengthen both communities and families.

Patricia Stone Motes
Peg McCartt Hess

Introduction

Communities and human service organizations can greatly support and strengthen the lives of families; however, they are often challenged in meeting these important tasks. During the past three decades, several developments have affected how communities and organizations are addressing this challenge. First, there has been a shift of focus from the individual to an ecological perspective, including attention to families, schools, neighborhoods, and other systems affecting individuals. This change in emphasis highlights an increased awareness of the importance of the family and other systems for an individual's development and functioning. The results are reciprocal in that positive influences from families and systems create strong individuals who make up strong families and, consequently, build a strong society.

Many agencies and organizations have implemented innovative family support programs in response, such as after-school programs, respite care, intensive home-based services, and mutual support parenting groups. At the same time, social science researchers began examining the ways in which neighborhoods and communities either support or hinder families' efforts to produce healthy individuals. As knowledge about community strengths and challenges has grown, the focus of human services has broadened to include the neighborhoods of the families served. Major governmental and private funders have consistently begun to call for programs to strengthen both communities and the families living in them.

Second, driven by a growing consensus from both private and public funders that community-based programming must be fiscally accountable and deliver positive program outcomes, family-serving organizations and community groups are being challenged to deliver outcomes at a higher standard. These challenges are occurring even as funding for community-based programming is becoming more limited. Thus, not only must programming meet higher standards, but programs must do so within an environment where resources to support families have become more limited.

Such changes have prompted many organizations and community groups to seek consultation, technical assistance, and specialized services from individuals, management-consultant firms, and university units such as institutes and centers. These partnerships offer support in areas such as strategic planning, program development, resource development, and program evaluation to advance the organization's efforts to serve the community and to be responsive to requirements of funders. In some instances, these partnerships provide that avenue for incorporating program development, program evaluation, and other supports into existing organizational infrastructures. However, the capacity to carry out these numerous accountability requirements is often beyond the capabilities of many community-based organizations and programs, and thus partnerships with consultants are often pragmatic choices for organizations and community groups.

This book reflects the experiences of a group of faculty members, researchers, and practitioners affiliated with the Institute for Families in Society, an interdisciplinary unit of the University of South Carolina that seeks to enhance the well-being of families through research, education, consultation, and technical assistance at community, state, national, and international levels. Institute faculty are from fields such as education, sociology, psychology, social work, public health, geography, nursing, law, medicine, women's studies, African American studies, and computer science. They represent a vast array of cultural backgrounds and professional and life experiences. While this book is grounded in research, it is also reflective of the lived experiences of the contributors.

As this book was being written, the institute was providing capacity-building consultation or technical assistance to more than 200 community-based organizations and institutions. A substantial portion of that work included evaluation support, organizational development activities, and the building of community coalitions and partnerships. As "coaches" or "capacity-building consultants,"[1]

---

1. The term "coach" encompasses many ways of offering support and facilitating action. As traditionally used in athletics, it refers to one who instructs players in the fundamentals of a sport and directs team strategy (e.g., a basketball coach). More recently, this term has taken on broader uses, where the term "coach" may refer to persons in multiple settings or fields (e.g., education, psychology, arts, medicine) who assist others in achieving specific goals (e.g.,

institute faculty and staff work as mediators (i.e., intermediaries effecting or facilitating change) to strengthen organizations and community groups, thus allowing these entities to increase their capacity to support and strengthen families.

Capacity building is not a simple process; it involves many tasks (e.g., reaching out to the community, building leadership, developing and planning for action) that require knowledge and skills. Participants in this community or organizational development process engage in numerous actions in support of these tasks, often with guidance from a consultant. Table 0.1 provides examples of tasks and the accompanying supportive actions.

In our experience as consultants providing capacity-building support, we believe the actions enumerated in table 0.1 are not separate and unique entities, occurring independently or in a specified step-wise progress. Rather, they are interdependent, interconnected, and iterative activities that support capacity building, and, as such, they provide the anchor for our work and this book.

In this book, we present a framework for organizational and community capacity building. We identify strategies and methods that are effective for consultants engaged in this work. Through vignettes and case examples,[2] we illustrate lessons learned by a team of consultants who assist a wide range of family-serving community organizations and groups. The conceptualization of the chapters grew out of a structured collaborative process wherein the editors and contributors met regularly to discuss and critically review their experiences and to develop the book's purpose, focus, and contents. Thus, whether chapters have one author or multiple authors, the work is accurately described as a collective of all of the contributors to this volume.

Chapter 1 lays the foundation for the importance of strong communities in the promotion of strong and healthy families. The authors address the needs of organizations and communities for capacity building to support families in their development and adaptation. The roles of the coach or capacity-building

---

life coach, drama coach, birthing coach). In *Empowerment evaluation: Knowledge and tools for self-assessment and accountability* (Fetterman, Kaftarian, and Wandersman, 1996), the term "coach" is introduced in reference to empowerment evaluators who facilitate others in conducting self-evaluation. Inherent in the coaching role is fostering improvement and self-determination—helping others help themselves. Throughout this volume, the term "coach" builds on the work of Fetterman and colleagues and refers to "capacity-building consultants" who provide technical assistance to community groups or organizations to support and strengthen families.

2. Where organizations are identified in vignettes and case examples, permission has been given. In all other vignettes and case examples, identities are disguised.

TABLE O.1 Building Organizational and Community Capacity

Tasks	Examples of Supportive Actions
Reaching out to the community (e.g., Chaskin et al., 2001; Floyd et al., 2003; Kreztmann and McKnight, 1993; Kubisch et al., 2002)	• Contact stakeholders • Include diverse groups • Build bridges across groups • Facilitate cultural competency • Build partnerships and collaboratives
Building leadership (e.g., Chaskin et al., 2001; Floyd et al., 2003; Kreztmann and McKnight, 1993; Kubisch et al., 2002)	• Develop decision-making process • Develop governance (e.g., board) • Develop organizational structure and functions • Assure stakeholder (e.g., family) leadership • Clarify roles and responsibilities • Develop executive function and staff capacity • Develop governance policies and procedures
Developing a plan for action (e.g., Brown, 1995; Fetterman, 2001; Fetterman, Kaftarian, and Wandersman, 1996; Linney and Wandersman, 1991)	• Assess assets and needs • Define scope of work • Choose effective practices that build on assets and address needs • Choose strategies • Design tactics • Document plan for action • Develop process to ensure that plan is followed (e.g., logic model)
Obtaining needed resources (e.g., Kreztmann and McKnight, 1993; Mattessich and Monsey, 1992; Rabin 1992)	• Assess resource potential (e.g., people, materials, funds) • Develop resource/business plan (budget) to support action • Secure needed resources • Develop sustainability plan
Building infrastructure (e.g., Mitchell, Florin and Stevenson, 2002; Andrews, Motes, Floyd, Flerx, and Lòpez-De Fede, 2005)	• Develop management plan • Develop and manage operational policies and procedures • Manage resources (e.g., personnel, finances, property) *(continued)*

TABLE O.I Building Organizational and Community Capacity (*continued*)

Tasks	Examples of Supportive Actions
Building infrastructure	• Facilitate teamwork (e.g., manage conflict, clarify roles) • Stimulate productivity • Assure quality (e.g., incorporation of evidence-based practices) • Manage information transfer and communication
Measuring success (e.g., Fetterman, 1994; Fetterman, Kaftarian, and Wandersman, 1996; Fetterman and Wandersman, 2004; Linney and Wandersman, 1991; Whitmore, 1990)	• Develop evaluation plan • Monitor progress toward intended outcomes • Review and respond to evaluative information • Reflect on and articulate lessons learned • Redesign action as appropriate • Assure accountability
Promoting sustainability (e.g., Kreztmann and McKnight, 1993; Mattessich and Monsey, 1992)	• Document capacity-building process and results • Disseminate information to stakeholders and public • Communicate success • Build on successes

consultant in facilitating the work of family-serving organizations and community groups are presented.

In chapter 2, the authors examine the related but distinct activities of consultation, technical assistance, and service. They present a conceptual framework for providing technical assistance, including the discussion of relevant theories, such as empowerment theory, adult learning theory and change theory. Principles and methods for providing technical assistance are offered. Emphasis is given to coaching as a useful strategy for the provision of technical assistance.

Although issues of cultural competence are integrated throughout the volume, chapter 3 focuses specifically on that topic, emphasizing that cultural competence is an essential component of the practice of consultation and technical assistance. The authors examine critical attitudes and actions that facilitate the development of cultural competence for professionals, organizations, and communities. They examine the ways in which consultants assist communities and organizations in providing culturally competent programs and services to families.

Chapter 4 points out that collaboration is both a highly valued strategy for community capacity building and a capacity-consuming process. This chapter reviews models for understanding and evaluating collaboratives, identifies dimensions of consultation and technical assistance to collaboratives, and describes both the capacity requirements for collaboration and the capacity-building benefits of collaboration.

Consultants are often called upon to support strategic planning efforts. Chapter 5 provides an overview of the strategic planning process with an emphasis on how to use this process to benefit community programs—not simply the development of a glossy document. This chapter builds upon the experiences of consultants who worked with the statewide school-readiness initiative in South Carolina.

Chapter 6 presents an approach to increase capacity for program self-evaluation for practitioners working with community-based agencies and organizations. The chapter describes the theoretical framework for this model of technical assistance. While the process of increasing an agency or program's capacity to perform self-evaluation is complex, this chapter presents step-by-step details for accomplishing this task.

When capacity-building efforts are successful, organizations and community groups are better able to support and strengthen families. The concluding chapter highlights significant themes that recur throughout the volume: clarity of expectations and roles, individualization of efforts, the complexity of the work, the need to balance diverse tensions, ethical mandates and dilemmas, and the demands inherent in organizational and community capacity building. While the demands are great, capacity building is a vital cornerstone for creating healthy families and building a strong society. We hope that this book encourages you to join us in that quest.

References

Andrews, A. B., Motes, P. S., Floyd, A. G., Flerx, V. C., and Lòpez–De Fede, A. (2005). Building evaluation capacity in community-based organizations: Reflections of an empowerment evaluation team. *Journal of Community Practice, 13* (4).

Brown, P. (1995). The role of the evaluator in comprehensive community initiatives. In J. P. Connell, A. C. Kubisch, L. B. Schorr, C. H. and Weiss (Eds.), *New approaches to evaluating community initiatives: Concepts, methods, and contexts* (pp. 201–25). Washington, D.C.: The Aspen Institute.

Chaskin, R. J., Brown, P., Venkatesh, S., and Vidal, A. (2001). *Building community capacity.* New York: Aldine de Gruyter.

Fetterman, D. (1994). Empowerment evaluation. *Evaluation Practice, 15* (1), 1–15.

Fetterman, D. (2001). Empowerment evaluation and self-determination: A practical approach toward program improvement and capacity building. In N. Schneiderman and M. A. Speers (Eds.), *Integrating behavioral and social sciences with public health* (pp. 321–50). Washington, D.C.: American Psychological Association.

Fetterman, D., Kaftarian, S., and Wandersman, A. (Eds.). (1996). *Empowerment evaluation: Knowledge and tools for self-assessment and accountability.* Thousand Oaks, Calif.: Sage.

Fetterman, D. M., and Wandersman, A. (Eds.). (2004). *Empowerment evaluation principles in practice.* New York: Guilford Publications.

Floyd, A. G., Andrews, A. B., Hess, P., Flerx, V. C., Rivers, J., Phillips, L., Whiting, J. A., Malson, M. R., and Kinnard, D. (2003). *Lessons learned and affirmed: The Duke Endowment Children and Families Program, final report.* Columbia, S.C.: University of South Carolina, Institute for Families in Society.

Kretzmann, J. P. and McKnight, J. L. (1993) *Building communities from the inside out: A path toward finding and mobilizing a community's assets.* Chicago: ACTA Publications.

Kubisch, A. C., Auspos, P., Brown, P., Chaskin, R., Fulbright-Anderson, K., and Hamilton, R. (2002). *Voices from the field II: Reflections on comprehensive community change.* Washington, D.C.: Aspen Institute.

Linney, J. A., and Wandersman, A. (Eds.). (1991). *Prevention plus III: Assessing alcohol and other drug prevention programs at the school and community level: A four step guide to useful program assessment.* Rockville, Md.: Office for Substance Abuse Prevention.

Mattessich, P. W., and Monsey, B. R. (1992). *Collaboration: What makes it work.* St. Paul, Minn.: Amherst H. Wilder Foundation.

Mitchell, R. E., Florin, P., and Stevenson, J. F. (2002). Supporting community-based prevention and health promotion initiatives: Developing effective technical assistance systems. *Health Education and Behavior, 29* (5), 620–39.

Rabin, S. (1992). Pooling resources builds private/public partnerships. *Public Relations Journal, 48* (10), 32–34.

Whitmore, E. (1990). Empowerment in program evaluation: A case example. *Canadian Social Work Review, 7* (2), 215–29.

Collaborating with Community-Based Organizations
Through Consultation and Technical Assistance

Chapter One

Organizational and Community Capacity Building

Mediating Change in Family-Serving Organizations and Groups

▓ ▓ ▓

ARLENE BOWERS ANDREWS AND PATRICIA STONE MOTES

Across the globe, communities and organizations are engaged in active efforts to promote healthy human development throughout the lifespan by strengthening families. In 1989 the United Nations heeded the advice of an interdisciplinary international panel of experts and declared, "The family is the basic unit of society" (United Nations, 1994). In a strong and healthy society, families care for members from the cradle to the grave and send forth individuals who weave the fabric of sustainable communities and organizations (i.e., communities and organizations that manage and maximize their resources to enhance and maintain the well-being of community members). They farm, build, teach, worship, explore, and provide support and resources that enable families to nurture their members.

When communities and organizations either fail to support families or actively interfere with a family's efforts to care for its members, social problems abound in the forms of crime, preventable illnesses, ignorance, and societal disintegration. When families have support, societies tend to be safe, healthy, creative, and cohesive. To this end, the UN initiative called on local communities and nations everywhere to seek ways to strengthen families, affirming that "the widest possible protection and assistance should be accorded to the family, which is the natural and fundamental unit of society" (United

Nations, 1966, article 10). The call emerged from a growing worldwide family support movement based on community and political action and involving all sectors of society. Some of this action succeeds, some fails, some plods along. Some is spontaneous, but increasingly, the action is, by design, facilitated by a growing cadre of professionals who help community groups and organizations plan, manage, and evaluate their actions. These professionals are termed "capacity-building consultants" or "coaches"[1] throughout this book.

A statement by Prudence Brown (1995) illustrates the diverse expectations communities and organizations have of a capacity-building consultant. Speaking of those who function as "evaluator," she notes that they are expected to play multiple roles: "scientist, judge, educator, technical assistant, facilitator, documenter/historian, and repository of institutional memory, coach, manager, planner, creative problem solver, co-learner, fundraiser, and public relations representative" (p. 201). Capacity-building consultants or coaches also serve as trainers, brokers, data gatherers, forecasters (i.e., predicting consequences of alternative courses of action), writers, and advisers. What they do not do is direct, decide, lead, or administer action. That is the domain of the participants in the process, those who belong to the community or organization.

Coaches in the family-support capacity-building movement occasionally share stories of challenges and celebrations through their professional associations and publications. By sharing lessons learned, they support one another's efforts to be effective and resource efficient. Documenting and disseminating information about the best, as well as the worst, of practices helps improve the technical assistance process and the results achieved by communities and organizations. This book is a compilation of experiences carried out by capacity-building consultants or coaches in various roles and settings designed to

1. The term "coach" encompasses many ways of offering support and facilitating action. As traditionally used in athletics, it refers to one who instructs players in the fundamentals of a sport and directs team strategy (e.g. basketball coach). More recently this term has taken on broader uses, where the term coach may refer to persons in multiple settings or fields (e.g., education, psychology, arts, medicine) who assist others in achieving specific goals (e.g., life coach, drama coach, birthing coach). In *Empowerment evaluation: Knowledge and tools for self-assessment and accountability* (Fetterman, Kaftarian, and Wandersman, 1996), the term "coach" is introduced in reference to empowerment evaluators who facilitate others in conducting self-evaluation. Inherent in the coaching role is fostering improvement and self-determination; helping others help themselves. Throughout this volume, the term coach builds on the work of Fetterman and colleagues and is used interchangeably with the term "capacity-building consultants" who provide technical assistance to community groups or organizations to support and strengthen families.

improve the family-support capacity of community groups and organizations. This chapter addresses the core themes that form the foundation of the work: the significance of strong families, organizational and community capacity building, and the roles of the capacity-building consultant or coach in facilitating family-community connections.

THE SIGNIFICANCE OF STRONG FAMILIES

Simply put, strong families produce the people who build strong societies. In a world moving toward widespread democracy in various forms, families become the breeding ground for responsible, contributing citizens. In the United States, families lay the foundation for an individual's ability to exercise rights of self-determination and freedom within a social context, respecting the rights of others. Families provide mutual support and promote resilience in times of struggle, helping individuals become resourceful members of their own community.

Discussions of family conditions often center on family structure, which has always changed according to adaptations necessary for particular cultural and historical contexts. Structurally, families may include grandparents (increasingly, of more than one generation), mothers, fathers, including gay and lesbian-headed households, children (including foster and adoptive), step-relatives, half-siblings, aunts, uncles, cousins, and people related by blood or marriage (current or former). Sometimes family members live together, sometimes in separate households. A particular family's composition changes periodically, but its basic functions are constant, as noted here:

> Far from being static, families are dynamic units engaged in an intertwined process of individual and group development. They can be seen as a biological unit whose members are linked together by blood ties; this relationship is often institutionalized through marriage or sanctioned by an equivalent relationship and describes the kinship between mothers, fathers, and their children. Secondly, a family can be seen as a social unit consisting of a number of people, who usually live together in the same household and share different developmental tasks and social functions. Thirdly, a family can be seen as a psychological unit defined around the personal feelings and emotional bonds of its members.
>
> (United Nations, 1994, p. 1)

As of the twenty-first century, families across the globe are changing more rapidly than at any other time in human history (Zeitlin, Megawangi,

Kramer, Colleta, Babatunde, and Garman, 1995). Evolving technology (e.g., Internet, diverse travel options) offers both the opportunity to sustain relationships across geographical boundaries and the opportunity to instantly build new ones. However, many of these new relationships are likely to be short-term relationships. Thus, adding to the growing demographics of fewer stable, long-term, close relationships (Baym, 1998, 2000; Wellman, 1997, 2001). A century ago, community change could be described in periods of human generations, whereas now communities grow and shrink dramatically in periods of just a few years and in some cases within months. Life in developed countries like the United States is complicated. Many families find themselves in shifting economies and changing neighborhoods with support from a variety of fragmented, specialized, and hardly accessible sources. Such social, political, and economic changes impose tremendous stresses that weaken families' abilities to care for their members (e.g., PolicyLink, 2002; Smedley and Syme, 2000).

Families with adequate internal resources manage, with relative ease, to garner not only what they need but also what they desire from their communities. Their lives may be troubled, but they generally can overcome access barriers and benefit from high-quality health care and education, fair access to justice, and other such privileges. Families who have been historically denied adequate resources or have become marginalized fare less well. They suffer the burden of disparities (PolicyLink, 2002). Many feel politically impotent, economically oppressed, and psychologically helpless in community arenas outside the comforting circle of their own family and friends. They struggle with unemployment or poor job conditions, discrimination, inferior schools, poor child care, poor care for older adults, and insufficient health care. Even when marginal groups gather strength, their more endowed neighbors tend to gather greater strength, and the relative disparities persist (e.g., Ceci and Papierno, 2005). This dynamic makes for fragile and fragmented communities rather than strong, sustainable communities.

Families derive their strength from internal resources such as communication and coping skills, affection, time together, shared beliefs, and cohesion, as well as external resources found within their social, economic, political, and physical environments (Voydanoff, Fine, and Donnelly, 1994; Zeitlin et al., 1995). Families look to their communities and organizations for support in the areas of

- material resources (e.g., food, clean water, shelter, clothing, health and hygiene supplies, transportation);

- education and developmental resources (e.g., early care and development resources, schools, moral guidance and character education, higher education, resources for people with disabilities, retirement planning, late-life resources);
- cultural and ethnic identity and understanding (e.g., public policy that recognizes differences, values differences, adapts to diversity);
- social and emotional support (e.g., psychological crisis assistance, mutual support and mentoring for life transitions, companionship);
- health and mental health care (e.g., availability and access to appropriate services);
- spirituality and faith-development resources (e.g., outreach services within and outside of memberships);
- justice resources (e.g., civil rights, victim rights, offender rights and responsibilities);
- physical safety (e.g., police protection, environments free from toxins, hazards, and blight); and
- economic resources (e.g., access to goods and services, jobs with adequate wages, job training and advancement opportunities).

The mythological self-sufficient family provides its members of various ages with all they need in the form of materials, education, developmental guidance, social and emotional support, spiritual guidance, justice, safety, and economic resources. This family, were it real, would send forth its members to contribute to certain aspects of society and return home to independently nurture and provide for their own. With possible rare exceptions, families do not function that way. They live interdependently with their neighbors and are powerfully influenced by their environments, whether by design or happenstance. These influences may be positive or negative. The goal of building organizational and community capacity for family support is to shift these forces in a positive direction.

ORGANIZATIONAL AND COMMUNITY CAPACITY BUILDING

After more than 200 years of sustained democracy, the United States still struggles to achieve full political and economic participation for its citizens, especially groups oppressed by policies and practices due to their class, race, gender, and ability. Historically, these groups have banded together for mutual support through informal and formal associations, particularly at the "grassroots" level (Garr, 1995). More privileged groups have had their associations, too, and have had greater influence over the collective institutions that govern and guide community life. As U.S. society has diversified and the ethic of intergroup harmony and tolerance has spread, historically oppressed groups have attained increasing political, economic, and social power. They have influenced the redirection of resources to local and grassroots organizations and community groups (Garr, 1995).

During the past three decades, social scientists have increasingly lent their wisdom to efforts aimed at strengthening communities and organizations. Sociologists, social workers, community psychologists, applied anthropologists, public health specialists, human rights lawyers, educators, management scientists, and political scientists have generated a substantial literature about the theory and practice of building communities and organizations. Much of the literature is ideological and theoretical, although recently more information reflects the effort to convert ideology to reality through effective action (Berger and Neuhaus, 1997; Strader, Collins, and Noe, 2000). Such action includes efforts that enhance the lives of people across the lifespan through pairing of older adults with middle school students (Kaplan, Henkin, and Kusano, 2002; Taylor and Bressler, 2000); increasing the ability of family members to better cope with work and family stress (Snow, Grady, Zimmerman, Puterski, Laughlin, and Pruett, 2004); and enhancing family functioning and reducing risk for substance abuse (McDonald and Frey, 1999). A broader effort is the "Healthy Cities and Communities" model promulgated by the World Health Organization, the International Healthy Cities Foundation, the U.S. Department of Health and Human Services, U.S. Coalition for Healthier Cities and Communities, and the W. K. Kellogg Foundation, which has resulted in formal efforts that include eighteen national networks in Europe, North America, and Australia; state efforts in the United States such as California Healthy Cities and Indiana Healthy Cities; several regional and language-specific networks; and a host of independent initiatives, including many spread across the developing world (Flower, 1996). The model involves various sectors of the community, including business, government, health, and faith communities, to address local needs and issues that include efforts that range from immunization drives to self-esteem classes to developing sewer systems. Further explicit tools have been developed to guide local efforts (for example, see Baker, Conrad, Be'champs, and Barry, 1999). The University of Kansas Community Toolbox (Francisco, Fawcett, Schultz, Berkowitz, Wolff, and Nagy, 2001) is among the leading research-based resources for practical guidance for individuals supporting community building, especially at the grassroots level.

DEFINING A FRAMEWORK FOR BUILDING
COMMUNITY CAPACITY

Professionals who support capacity-building efforts with community groups and organizations come from various disciplinary fields and cultural perspectives and, at present, use no widely accepted standard language. The following terms, noted in italics, incorporate many elements that are common in various definitions and are offered here as a conceptual foundation for topics discussed in this chapter and throughout this book.

Communities are essentially groups of people who share interests or attributes and relate to one another in ways that meet needs, address common goals, or provide meaning. "Community" is a general term that may refer to a place, an ideal, or a social network. For example, people may refer to their county as a community, to the "faith community" (referring in general to people who are active in faith-based congregations), or to the community of parents whose children have disabilities. When a community shares a common space within a geographic area, it may be known as a neighborhood or broader geographic community. "Geographic community" (Fellin, 1987; Rothenbuhler, 1995) typically refers to a social group that

- shares space,
- interacts in predictable ways,
- shares a collective perception of group boundaries (that is, who is in and who is out),
- shares collective identity, and
- shares feelings of belonging.

Organizations range from the informal association to the highly complex formal bureaucracy (Hasenfeld, 1992; Hatch, 1997; Hesselbein, Goldsmith, Backhard, and Drucker, 1997). An organization generally has a purpose, a structure, norms about functioning, and resources. The informal organization is a loose affiliation among people who operate flexibly, often with fluid participation. "Grassroots" organizations, those that are built by local people using their own resources, often fall into this category, although organizations tend to move toward formality over time (Kahn, 1991). At the other extreme is the well-defined formal organization with a clearly articulated mission, fixed structure, and rules about functions. Organizations are the vehicles through which communities and groups within communities act together.

Capacity, as related to community, is captured in this definition offered by Chaskin, Brown, Verkatesh, and Vidal (2001):

> Community capacity is the interaction of human capital, organizational resources, and social capital existing within a given community that can be leveraged to solve collective problems and improve or maintain the well-being of that community. It may operate through informal social processes and/or organized efforts by individuals, organizations, and social networks that exist among them and between them and the larger systems of which the community is a part. (p. 7)

Putnam (1993) defines social capital as "features of social organization, such as networks, norms, trust, that facilitate coordination and cooperation for benefit" (p. 36). Essentially, community capacity can be regarded as the assets and processes that a community brings to the process of developing community well-being or mutual benefit. Capacity is both a means and an end, in that it is constantly evolving as part of a dynamic environment.

Capacity building is planned intervention to expand, enrich, or otherwise improve capacity. This may require, for example, enhanced capital or resources, altered interactions among community members, or improved member attitudes, knowledge, or skills. The building process tends to be facilitated by those who know the community best with assistance from skilled resource persons who can offer expertise regarding specific asset development or process facilitation.

Community and organizational capacity building for stronger families is the planned process of community-asset development for the purpose of improving or maintaining family well-being. This process recognizes that families depend on communities and organizations to support them in multiple ways and that many communities are characterized by families that have limited internal and external resources. Sustainable capacity-building efforts, however, must build upon the strengths and competencies of families, not simply needs, if effective community and organizational capacity building is to occur. The skills, abilities, capacities, and assets of all families are essential to defining issues, solving problems, and mobilizing and sustaining change for the well-being of families (Kretzman and McKnight, 1993).

At the local level, community and organizational capacity building tend to blend. As Lisbeth Schorr (1997) points outs, successful programs are not just *in* but also *of* the community (p. 8). Schorr notes that community programs that succeed in solving social problems, such as child abuse, youth violence, and intergenerational poverty, tend to be small and scarce rather than embraced by everyone and widely promulgated. Their participants feel a sense of ownership and belonging. Coaches to the capacity-building process may not be of the community, but they must be competent in relating to the unique culture and attributes of the community and respectful of the community's control of the process and outcomes.

Ecologically, family outcomes are influenced by factors in the larger society (such as laws, popular culture, social norms, global economic trends) and neighborhood conditions (such as the local economy, demography, physical environment). The influence of these societal factors and conditions is mediated by factors such as the neighborhood's sense of collective efficacy, social capital, and organizational effectiveness—informal and formal (Massey, 2001; Sampson, 2001). Most planned intervention to promote community and organizational capacity building is directed at changing these local mediating factors. Thus, the work does not involve "direct services" to individuals or families. Rather, it involves helping family-serving organizations to lead or participate in efforts to improve the mediating factors. The effort also requires changes in institutional processes, which typically requires interventions with policymakers, media, and business leadership sectors. Thus, as coaches to this process, we are working to increase the capacity of local groups and organizations to impact these mediating factors.

Chaskin et al. (2001) illustrate the complexity of building community and organizational capacity by offering a comprehensive, multidimensional definitional framework. They identify three dimensions of community capacity:

- fundamental characteristics (e.g., sense of community, commitment, ability to solve problems, access to resources);
- levels of social agency (individual, organizational, network); and
- the community's particular functions (planning/governance, production of goods and services, information dissemination, organizing and advocacy)

(pp. 11–12).

Their framework includes typical strategies that are used to promote community strength, such as leadership development, organizational development, organizing, and interorganizational collaboration. Another core dimension is the context in which the community exists, which includes the influences that support or inhibit capacity. And finally, the framework incorporates outcomes, the indicators of the success of the capacity-building process.

THE COACH'S ROLE IN FACILITATING
FAMILY-COMMUNITY CONNECTIONS

As coaches to family-serving organizations and groups, we work to strengthen organizations and communities through technical assistance, thus allowing organizations and community groups to increase their capacity to strengthen families. Inherent in the coaching role is a deliberate focus on fostering improvement and self-determination; helping others help themselves (Fetterman, Kaftarian, and Wandersman, 1996). As coaches we rarely work directly with families but rather with mediating organizations (e.g., community-based organizations, nongovernmental and public agencies, social action groups). As presented in the introductory chapter, the capacity-building process involves many tasks (e.g., reaching out to the community, building leadership, measuring success) that require knowledge and skills. As coaches, we find ourselves working with participants in the community or organization as they engage in numerous actions in support of these tasks. An understanding of the influence of mediating factors (social supports, community readiness, accessibility of program services, etc.) is essential to the coaching process.

Capacity-building consultants promote leadership, providing support on such matters as policy issues, organizational governance and management, and eliciting the capabilities of family caregivers and consumers as leaders in the community and organizational action. They offer support on a host of organizational development activities, such as planning and evaluation, research-based effective practices, staff development, fundraising and planning for sustainability, financial accountability, public and media relations, personnel administration, and information management. They advise regarding organizing practices and full participation, including cultural competence, inclusively building bridges across various sectors of the community, and accommodating differences. Further, they facilitate broad community coalitions and interorganizational relations.

Democratic Participation and Empowerment

A principle that guides technical assistance with communities and organizations is that of democratic participation, which often requires empowerment of historically excluded populations. While there is no standard approach to an operational definition of empowerment, the seminal work of Barbara Solomon (1976) offers the anchor for much of its current use. When Solomon originally coined the term "empowerment," she was describing the actions of disenfranchised African Americans as they became a significant force in shaping political ideology and resources that affected the quality of their lives. Building on the work of Solomon, the following personal and collective empowerment themes recur among scholars in the field:

- *Personal empowerment* is associated with personal freedom, self-determination, self-esteem, personal control, personal responsibility, perceived competence, and self-efficacy (Bandura, 1997; Peterson, Hamme, and Speer, 2002; Rappaport, 1984, 1987; Solomon, 1976, 1987). The empowered person exercises choice, acts accordingly, and believes chosen actions can attain desired results.
- *Collective empowerment* through organizations and community groups involves active, inclusive participation in group decision making, social responsibility, mutual support among participants, and group capacity building. Empowered groups and organizations plan, enact, and evaluate interventions that affect their collective group. The collective may range from small to quite large, such as a single interpersonal relationship, a support group, an organization, or mass political action (Israel, Checkoway, Schulz, and Zimmerman, 1994; Rappaport, 1984, 1987; Solomon, 1976, 1987; Wallerstein and Bernstein, 1994).

The process of empowerment for historically excluded or oppressed populations requires transformation (i.e., mobilization by these populations around their own self-defined interests) (Friere, 1973; Solomon, 1976, 1987). At the same time, empowerment involves those that have experienced relative privilege to act in ways that enable, support, or at least do not hinder the empowerment of others (Friere, 1973; Gutiérrez, DeLois, and GlenMaye, 1995). The sharing of political power is a cornerstone of democracy and a value that drives the move toward empowerment. People create or are given opportunities to exercise control and influence. As Sprague and Hayes (2000) note, "To empower someone is to facilitate their self-determination. Empowering relationships are constructed on both interpersonal and social structural levels. The reason some of us are self-determining is that we are in interpersonal and social structural relationships that empower us" (p. 681).

Where families are at risk or suffer deficiencies in community supports, shifting power relations becomes an essential part of the community capacity-building process. This makes for complex, challenging work. Capacity-building consultants must be aware of their power, real and as perceived by themselves and others. Typically, the power of these consultants comes from the auspices through which they are providing the work (e.g., their funders) and their expertise, authority, and professional associations. They must also observe power dynamics within the community or organization and be prepared to manage conflict and assist negotiation. Nurturing communication skills and structures that build a foundation for future problem solving as well as addressing immediate concerns makes for long-term commitments, stability, and sustainable processes within the community.

Himmelman (2001) differentiates "betterment" initiatives from "empowerment" initiatives, noting the former are more externally controlled or influenced by a funding organization or "lead" agency, whereas the latter are driven by community members. While empowerment is the democratic ideal and the goal of most coaches, reality dictates that at times, betterment is the feasible alternative. In either case, inclusive participation can be realized. House and Howe (2000), though focused on evaluation, offer ten questions to guide democratic participation that are relevant to other capacity-building processes:

1. Whose interests are represented?
2. Are major stakeholders represented?
3. Are any stakeholders excluded?
4. Are there serious power imbalances?
5. Are there procedures for controlling the imbalances?
6. How do people participate in the evaluation?
7. How authentic is their participation?
8. How involved are they?
9. Is there reflective deliberation?
10. How considered and extended is the deliberation?

(pp. 10–11).

Strong participation and collaboration increases the chances that an effective change process will be sustained within a community group or organization. External resources, such as grants from the state or federal government or foundations, initiate many change efforts. Often, these are time-limited investments, designed to produce a specific result while stimulating changes in the community or organizational infrastructure so that, if effective, the change can be sustained. A sustainable initiative will survive and thrive through changes in leadership, resources, and environmental transition (Barnett, Beurden, Eakin, Beard, Dietrich, and Newman, 2004; Marek, Mancini, Earthman, and Brock, 2003; Shediac-Rizkallah and Bone, 1998). Sustainable initiatives draw from local support in the form of continually replenished person power, physical resources, interpersonal relationships, and other essential resources.

Sharing Lessons Learned About Capacity Building

Building community capacity is considered both a process and a product. As a process, capacity building is an ongoing effort that includes communities assessing their strengths and needs and deciding upon a course of action to tackle what is necessary. As an end product, capacity building involves efforts that lead to certain outcomes, such as developing and sustaining services that meet the needs of older adults, improved after school programs for youth, or enhanced skills of the community members so that they are better able to tackle community issues now or in the future. In either instance, building community capacity involves strategies that help communities to use or enrich local resources to improve or sustain the well-being of the community (Chaskin et al., 2001).

The goal of capacity-building efforts is to create a community empowered to address its needs and move toward the development of a sustained community effort that addresses the well-being of its citizenry. Families are stronger when organizations and community groups work specifically to address the needs of families by building on their assets, with families as partners and collaborators to this process. Sharing lessons learned through community work strengthens these efforts.

Community capacity-building consultants work indirectly with communities through the facilitation of efforts by community groups and organizations. As mediators to family-strengthening processes, we support capacity-building efforts through the provision of a wide array of technical assistance. This technical assistance is provided to a range of persons (e.g., program staff, community members, evaluation team, board members, program directors) with goals that include support for organizational management, leadership skills, and resource development, support for the building of collaboratives, and the use of evaluation strategies to both improve programs and support accountability efforts. The efforts of the capacity-building consultant ultimately support the fundamental characteristics of communities with capacity as described by Chaskin and associates (2001):

1. a sense of community (connectedness among members and recognition of mutuality of circumstance);
2. a level of commitment among community members (community members as stakeholders and active participants in working for collective well-being);

3. mechanisms of problem solving (skills to translate commitment into action); and
4. access to diverse resources (e.g., economic, physical, political) beyond the neighborhood.

Through our capacity-building efforts with family-serving organizations and groups, we have come to know that capacity building for family strengthening is not easy but is indeed worthwhile to pursue. Whether programs are successful or challenged in reaching desired outcomes, families are strengthened as community members set goals of improving or maintaining the well-being of the community.

Clearly community and organizational work is hard labor. Capacity-building consultants must carefully tend the substance and process, like the gardener who must carefully design the garden so plants will coexist, repeatedly till the soil, add water and nutrients, and pull weeds. The work is neither quick nor simple. Science informs the process, but only close familiarity and practice wisdom can address the unique characteristics of a particular microenvironment. When the community or organization is well planned and nourished, its fruits will be strong, healthy, and sustainable.

CONCLUSIONS

Throughout the world, building sustainable community and organizational capacity for strengthening families depends upon democratic, empowered participation by all members of society. To overcome the historic exclusion of many groups, capacity-building consultants trained in various disciplines, supported by nongovernmental and public resources, work in numerous arenas to help shift power and resources in ways that promote inclusion and leadership from all sectors.

The year 2004 marked the tenth anniversary of the United Nation's declaration of the International Year of the Family. In a resolution calling for observation of this anniversary, the U.N. General Assembly recognized that continuing international efforts are needed to strengthen and support families as they perform their societal and developmental functions, in particular at the national and local levels. The assembly noted that a particular strategy is to enhance the effectiveness of local, national, and regional efforts to carry out specific programs concerning families, generate new activities, and strengthen existing ones. To this end, practitioners and researchers must share their lessons learned (i.e., what works, what doesn't work, and the uncertainties) as we move forward with a common vision to build organizational community capacity that strengthens families.

References

Baker, S., Conrad, D., Be'champs, M., and Barry, M. (1999). *Healthy people 2010 toolkit: A field guide to health planning.* Washington, D.C.: U.S. Dept. of Health and Human Services/Public Health Foundation.

Bandura, A. (1997). *Self-efficacy: The exercise of control.* New York: W. H. Freeman.

Berger, P. L. and Neuhaus, R. J. (1997). *To empower people: From state to civil society* (2nd ed.). Washington, DC: The Enterprise Institute Press.

Barnett, L. M., Beurden, E. V., Eakin, E. G., Beard, J. Dietrich, U., and Newman, B. (2004). Program sustainability of a community-based intervention to prevent falls among older Australians, *Health Promotion International, 19* (3), 281–88.

Baym, N. K. (1998) The emergence of on-line community. In S.G. Jones (Ed.), *CyberSociety 2.0: Revisiting computer-mediated communication and community* (pp. 35–68). Newbury Park, Calif.: Sage Publications.

Baym, N. K. (2000). *Tune in, log on: Soaps, fandom, and on-line community.* New York: Sage Publications.

Brown, P. (1995). The role of the evaluator in comprehensive community initiatives. In J. P. Connell, A. C. Kubisch, L. B. Schorr, and C. H. Weiss (Eds.), *New approaches to evaluating community initiatives: Concepts, methods, and contexts* (pp. 201–25). Washington, D.C.: The Aspen Institute.

Ceci, S. J. and Papierno, P. B. (2005). The rhetoric and reality of gap-closing: When the "have-nots" gain but the "haves" gain even more. *American Psychologist, 60,* 149–160.

Chaskin, R. J., Brown, P., Venkatesh, S., and Vidal, A. (2001). *Building community capacity.* New York: Aldine de Gruyter.

Fellin, P. (1987). *The community and the social worker.* Itasca, Ill.: F. E. Peacock.

Fetterman, D., Kaftarian, S., and Wandersman, A. (Eds.). (1996). *Empowerment evaluation: Knowledge and tools for self-assessment and accountability.* Thousand Oaks, Calif.: Sage.

Flower, J. (1996). Examples of healthier communities projects. Retrieved January 14, 2005, from the changeproject.com Web site at http://www.well.com/user/bbear/hc_examples.html.

Francisco, V. T., Fawcett, S. B., Schultz, J. A., Berkowitz, B., Wolff, T. J., and Nagy, G. (2001). Using Internet-based resources to build community capacity: The community tool box. *American Journal of Community Psychology, 29* (2), 293–300.

Friere, P. (1973). *Pedagogy of the oppressed.* New York: Seabury.

Garr, R. (1995). *Reinvesting in America: The grassroots movements that are feeding America and putting Americans back to work.* Boston, Mass.: Addison-Wesley.

Gutiérrez, L., DeLois, K., and GlenMaye, L. (1995). Understanding empowerment practice: Building on practitioner-based knowledge. *Families in Society, 76* (9), 534–42.

Hasenfeld, Y. (1992). *Human services as complex organizations.* Newbury Park, Calif.: Sage.

Hatch, M. J. (1997). *Organization theory: Modern, symbolic, and postmodern perspectives*. New York: Oxford University Press.

Hesselbein, F., Goldsmith, M., Backhard, R., and Drucker, P. (Eds.). (1997). *The organization of the future* (Drucker Foundation Future Series). San Francisco: Jossey-Bass.

Himmelman, A. T. (2001). On coalitions and the transformation of power relations: Collaborative betterment and collaborative empowerment. *American Journal of Community Psychology, 29* (2), 277–84.

House, E. R. and Howe, K. R. (2000). Deliberative democratic evaluation. *New Directions for Evaluation, 85*, 3–12.

Israel, B. A., Checkoway, B., Schulz, A., and Zimmerman, M. (1994). Health education and community empowerment: Conceptualizing and measuring perceptions of individual, organizational, and community control. *Health Education Quarterly, 21* (2), 149–70.

Kaplan, M., Henkin, N., and Kusano, A. (Eds.). (2002). *Linking lifetimes: A global view of intergenerational exchange*. Lanham, Md.: University Press of America.

Kahn, S. (1991). *Organizing: A guide for grassroots leaders* (rev. ed.). Washington, D.C.: National Association of Social Workers.

Kretzmann, J. P. and McKnight, J. L. (1993) *Building communities from the inside out: A path toward finding and mobilizing a community's assets*. Chicago: ACTA Publications.

Marek, L. I., Mancini, J. A., Earthman, G. E., and Brock, D. P. (2003). Ongoing community-based program implementation, successes, and obstacles: The National Youth at Risk Program Sustainability Study, Publication Number 350-804. Retrieved October 3, 2004, from Virginia Tech University, Virginia Cooperative Extension Web site: http://www.ext.vt.edu/pubs/family/350-804/350-804.html.

Massey, D. (2001). The prodigal paradigm returns: Ecology comes back to sociology. In A.Booth, and A. C. Crouter (Eds.), *Does it take a village? Community effects on children, adolescents, and families* (pp. 41–47). Mahwah, N.J.: Lawrence Erlbaum.

McDonald, L., and Frey, H. E. (1999). Families and schools together: Building relationships. *OJJDP Bulletin*. Washington, D.C.: U.S. Department of Justice, Office of Justice Programs, Office of Juvenile Justice and Delinquency Prevention.

Peterson, N. A., Hamme, C. L., and Speer, P. W. (2002). Cognitive empowerment of African Americans and Caucasians: Differences in understandings of power, political functioning, and shaping ideology. *Journal of Black Studies, 32* (3), 336–51.

PolicyLink. (2002). Reducing health disparities through a focus on communities. *PolicyLink*. Oakland, Calif.

Putnam, R. (1993, Spring). The prosperous community: Social capital and community life. *The American Prospect*, pp. 35–42.

Rappaport, J. (1984). Studies in empowerment: Introduction to the issue. In J.Rappaport, C. F. Swift, and R. E. Hess (Eds.), *Studies in empowerment* (pp. 1–7). New York: Haworth Press.

Rappaport, J. (1987). Terms of empowerment/exemplars of prevention: Toward a theory for community psychology. *American Journal of Community Psychology, 15* (2), 121–48.

Rothenbuhler, E. W. (1995). Understanding and constructing community: A communication approach. In P. Adams and K. Nelson (Eds.), *Reinventing human services: Community- and family-centered practice* (pp. 207–21). New York: Aldine de Gruyter.

Sampson, R. J. (2001). How do communities undergird or undermine human development? Relevant contexts and social mechanisms. In A. Booth and A. C. Crouter (Eds.), *Does it take a village? Community effects on children, adolescents, and families* (pp. 3–30). Mahwah, N.J.: Lawrence Erlbaum.

Schorr, L. B. (1997). *Common purpose: Strengthening families and neighborhoods to rebuild America.* New York: Anchor Books.

Shediac-Rizkallah, M. C. and Bone, L. R. (1998). Planning for the sustainability of community-based health programs: Conceptual frameworks and future directions for research, practice and policy. *Health Education Research: Theory and Practice, 13* (1), 87–108.

Smedley, B. D., and Syme, S. L. (Eds.). (2000). *Promoting health: Intervention strategies from social and behavioral research.* Washington, D.C.: National Academy Press.

Snow, D. L., Grady, K., Zimmerman, S. O., Puterski, D., Laughlin, P., and Pruett, M. K. (2004). Coping with work and family stress: A workplace preventive intervention. New Haven: Yale University School of Medicine, The Consultation Center, Department of Psychiatry, pp. 1–65.

Solomon, B. (1976). *Black empowerment: Social work in oppressed communities.* New York: Columbia University Press.

Solomon, B.B. (1987). Empowerment: Social work in oppressed communities. *Journal of Social Work Practice, 2* (4), 79–91.

Sprague, J., and Hayes, J. (2000). Self-determination and empowerment: A feminist standpoint analysis of talk about disability. *American Journal of Community Psychology, 28* (5), 671–95.

Strader, T. N., Collins, D. A. and Noe, T. D. (2000). *Building healthy individuals, families, and communities: Creating lasting connections.* (Prevention in Practice Library). Boston, Mass.: Plenum.

Taylor, A. and Bressler, J. (2000). *Mentoring across generations: Partnerships for positive youth development.* New York: Kluwer Academic/Plenum Press.

United Nations. (1994). *Guide for a national action programme on the International Year of the Family.* New York: Author.

United Nations. (1966). The International Covenant on Economic, Social and Cultural Rights. U.N. General Assembly resolution 220 A (XXI), annex, article 10.

Voydanoff, P., Fine, A. A., and Donnelly, B. (1994). Family structure, family organization, and quality of family life. *Journal of Family and Economic Issues, 15,* 175–200.

Wallerstein, N., and Bernstein, E. (1994). Introduction to community empowerment, participatory education, and health. Special issue of *Health Education Quarterly, 21* (2), 141–48.

Wellman B. (1997). An electronic group is virtually a social network. In S. Kiesler (Ed.), *Culture of the internet* (pp. 179–205). Mahwah, N.J.: Lawrence Erlbaum Associates.

Wellman B. (2001). Physical space and cyberspace: The rise of personalized networking. *International Journal of Urban and Regional Research, 25* (2), 227–52.

Zeitlin, M. F., Megawangi, R., Kramer, E. M., Colletta, N. D., Babatunde, E. D., and Garman, D. (1995). *Strengthening the family: Implications for international development.* New York: United Nations University Press.

Zimmerman, B. J. (2000). Self-efficacy: An essential motive to learn. *Contemporary Educational Psychology, 25* (1), 82–91.

Chapter Two

Consulting to Organizations and Community Groups

Defining and Distinguishing the Provision of Technical Assistance

■ ■ ■

PATRICIA STONE MOTES, JUDITH ANN WHITING,
AND JEANNINE P. SALONE

Consultants emerge from various milieus, such as government, private sector, and university settings. In general, the distinguishing characteristic of a consultant is expertise in a field or a skill that is not readily available to others who need it (e.g., Block, 1981; Schein, 1987). While consultants from all sectors are involved in capacity-building work with organizations and communities, academics and researchers in university settings, such as the contributors to this volume, are often selected as consultants because of access to state-of-the-art knowledge and technology. Most academicians are scholars in a particular field and their workplace, the academy, both expects and rewards the building of knowledge and the dissemination of that knowledge to constituents within and external to the academy. One of the most gratifying ways to share the fruits of this learning is by providing consultation, technical assistance, and service to communities and organizations. These activities also provide opportunities to test hypotheses and challenge accepted notions of reality.

The term "consultant" typically refers to an expert or professional, external to the contractor (e.g., agency, organization), who is hired to provide consultation or technical assistance (Block, 1981). A consultant also may be hired to provide services. *Thus a consultant may provide consultation, technical assistance, or services.* However, "consultation" and "technical assistance" describe the primary work consultants perform with organizations and community groups. These terms are often used interchangeably, as though they involve the same level of work. This chapter reflects our experience that consultation and technical assistance are related but distinct, varying in degree and kind. The boundaries between the two roles are sometimes nebulous, especially in practice, and consultants themselves may wonder if they are providing consultation or technical assistance. Differentiating between these tasks is essential. Both contractors and consultants need to understand these differences when negotiating performance expectations. Problems arise, for example, when a contract is negotiated for consultation, but technical assistance is what the agency really expected.

The approach presented in this chapter places consultation, technical assistance, and service on a continuum of supportive actions and tasks, where consultation typically involves indirect support of tasks, and service involves the most direct support. For example, a professional providing consultation may influence actions or tasks by giving information or advice (e.g., what items to include in an annual report), while the professional providing service will perform the task (e.g., write the annual report). Technical assistance involves more tangible involvement than giving of advice but less than the full performance of the task. Each of these three tasks differs in several ways, such as the degree of responsibility or accountability for tasks, the degree to which one has authority to compel action, and the level of involvement in decision making. For example, it is expected that professionals (i.e., consultants) hired to provide outsourced services will make multiple and varied decisions (e.g., executive, program management, case services), while professionals hired to provide consultation will not make decisions for organizations to which they are consulting. The degree of responsibility, authority, or influence for tasks or actions increases as the consultant's work moves from consultation through technical assistance and then into service.

In this chapter we provide a conceptual framework for technical assistance. Particular attention is given to coaching[1] as one useful strategy for the provision of technical assistance, and to the principles and limits of technical assistance. We also emphasize the relationships among technical assistance, consultation, and service and the knowledge, values, and skills required in providing technical assistance. Throughout this chapter, we present examples of technical assistance activities.

---

1. Throughout this volume, the term "coach" in used interchangeably with the term "capacity-building consultants" who provide technical assistance to community groups or organizations to support and strengthen families. Inherent in the coaching role is fostering improvement and self-determination; helping others help themselves.

DEFINITIONS

A quick Web search reveals numerous entries for "technical assistance and consultation." Typical of such entries is a tendency to use the terms interchangeably, as though each encompasses the other. For example, typical listings include one that defines consultation and technical assistance as a singular "collaborative process" (Networks for Training and Development, n.d., para. 1); one with a questionnaire that assesses satisfaction with the entity "technical assistance and consultation" (Moorhouse, 2002, p. 23); and others citing organizations that provide "consultation and technical assistance" activities, such as advocacy, strategic planning, grant proposal development, and evaluation (University of North Carolina, n.d., para. 1; Vroon Vandenberg, n.d., para. 2).

None of these either differentiated between technical assistance and consultation or identified factors that defined them. Within the professional literature, there is a growing volume of work that describes the significant level of effort involved in providing technical assistance, especially to organizations and communities with goals of capacity building (Aspen Institute, 2002; Brown, Pitt, and Hirota, 1999; Chavis, Florin, and Felix, 1993; Mitchell, Florin, and Stevenson, 2002; Trohanis, 2001). While the literature implies a distinction between technical assistance and consultation, this distinction is often not made explicit. However, our work with communities has convinced us that there are important differences that need to be made explicit between these activities and tasks. It is with these differences in mind that we propose the following working definitions.

Consultation. Consultation is the act or process of giving expert or professional advice, usually regarding some kind of problem or demand confronting an organization or community. In general, consultation involves reviewing a specific entity, such as a process, practice, or proposal, and giving an opinion about it (e.g., Block, 1981; Schein, 1987). For this review, the consultant relies principally on documents provided by the contractor, such as strategic plans, procedure and policy manuals, and reports, and on interviews with the contractor and its agents (e.g., employees), constituents (e.g., clients, customers, or members) and affiliates (e.g., community partners or other agency consultants). At the conclusion of this review, the consultant reports his or her findings and recommendations—in writing, verbally, or both—to the contractor.

Ongoing consultation may be provided, during which a consultant may review numerous aspects of an agency or organization. Regardless of how often or for how long a consultant is employed by the organization, consultation is limited to reviewing, reporting observations, and making recommendations specific to the subject of the consultation. Strong observation and interviewing skills are important for consultants doing this level of work, as they are in providing technical assistance and service. Examples of consultation include but are not limited to the analysis or assessment and recommendations regarding information systems, resources and needs, conflict and its resolution, personnel management, and clinical interventions.

Technical assistance. A consultant hired to provide technical assistance is expected to offer concrete and tangible help or support, such as modeling or training, for a specific purpose (e.g., Aspen Institute, 2002; Bruner, 1993; Mitchell et al., 2002; Trohanis, 2001; Wahl, Cahill, and Fruchter, 1998). This level of support is more involved than consultation; it often builds on the findings of an earlier consultation (e.g., recommendations for specific programmatic changes). The strength of technical assistance arises from (a) specialized knowledge and skills that are (b) grounded in theory, research, and practice and (c) adapted to a specific function or environment (Mitchell et al., 2002; Trohanis, 2001). Technical assistance typically includes but generally is more comprehensive than consultation. In fact, before effective technical assistance can be given, the consultant may find it necessary to engage in a systematic review of the organization or community in the same way a consultant does when providing consultation. At the conclusion of a consultation contract, the consultant may help the organization implement these recommendations. It is at this point that the role of the consultant shifts from providing consultation to either providing technical assistance or outsourced services.

Technical assistance takes many forms and serves many functions. For example, technical assistance may be provided by the staff of funding organizations as a resource to grantees, or consultants contracted by the funder may provide technical assistance to grantees. However, technical assistance is not always dependent on relationships between external funders and community organizations. It may be initiated by the community entity interested in enhancing its programs and or operations. One individual may provide technical assistance, or multiple individuals or teams may provide this support. Whether focusing on process issues (e.g., governance, board development, strategic planning) or on programmatic or content issues (e.g., service provisions, use of assessment measures, best practices research), technical assistance is designed to support the individual needs of each organization or community (Aspen Institute, 2002; Trohanis, 2001).

The discussion in this chapter and throughout this volume is largely built upon our experiences as a team of consultants contracted by external funders to support capacity-building efforts. In most cases, both the grantee and our team (i.e., capacity-building consultants or coaches) have been funded by the same entity. We have provided technical assistance through funding from the federal government, diverse state agencies, foundations, and nonprofits. In our role as coaches, we have worked as an "intermediary support organization" (Mitchell et al., 2002) to assist community-based organizations in their efforts to strengthen the capacity of communities and the families within these communities.

The following list includes some examples of technical assistance our team has provided:

- facilitation of organizational transitions (e.g., training a new advisory board, restructuring of client services, developing strategic plans);
- conflict resolution within collaboratives, mediation between funder and grantee, increasing access to services by diverse constituencies, developing management information systems, and facilitating data collection and data analysis;
- training (e.g., board development, cultural competence for agency staff, evaluation skills development); and
- supporting project teams to develop, implement, and evaluate initiatives.

Services. The provision of actual services to help an agency or organization achieve its objectives involves the greatest degree of responsibility, accountability, and authority given to a consultant by a contractor. This is often referred to as outsourcing. In this arrangement, it can be easy for the consultant to be mistaken as an employee of the agency because the consultant will be highly visible within and, perhaps, outside the agency. The following are examples of service provision:

- writing or preparing documents for agencies and programs,
- constructing databases,
- collecting data,
- entering data into a database,
- analyzing data,
- lobbying,
- interviewing applicants, and
- hiring or participating in other personnel decisions.

DIFFERENTIATING CONSULTATION, TECHNICAL ASSISTANCE, AND SERVICE ACTIONS SUPPORTIVE TO BUILDING CAPACITY

Community groups and organizations engage in many actions in support of capacity building (see table 0.1, in the introduction). These activities are often best supported by a team of consultants who work together, blending expertise, skills, and experiences to facilitate the growth of organizations and community groups. The supportive actions for key tasks (e.g., reaching out to the community, building leadership, obtaining needed resources) may involve consultation, technical assistance, or service. For example, when reaching out to the community, consultation with an organization may involve reviewing existing documents (e.g., brochures, newsletters, employee handbooks, employee rosters, salaries by race and gender), observing events or processes (e.g., board meetings, staff interactions, office furnishings and decorations) and making recommendations to the organization about how these materials may be perceived by diverse groups.

In the role of technical assistance provider, support for reaching out to the community might include coaching the organization in establishing a process to enhance cultural competency. The TA provider might support the organization by locating training materials appropriate for the organization's needs or by providing training on cultural competency to staff members and board members. In a different situation, the TA provider might work with the organization to build a community collaborative (e.g., providing needed support to ensure diverse constituencies are active participants).

Reaching out to the community could also involve consultant activities at the service level. For example, the consultant might be hired to provide a specific service to the organization, such as creating a database by constituent groups to support collaborative building efforts; serving as the multicultural coordinator to ensure that a diverse team is put in place for a specific project; writing an employee handbook; or writing policies and procedures that reflect cultural competency.

Given the needs of the organization or group, the consultant may offer consultation, technical assistance, or service. However, the degree of responsibility, authority, and decision making involved in each of these tasks is important to defining expectations, contracts, and the behavior of the professional who enters into a relationship with community members, organizational leaders, and funders. A professional who is hired to provide consultation on the best ways to develop cultural competence in an organization but actually establishes policies and procedures for ensuring cultural competency and writes the new procedures manual for the organization has clearly moved from the task of consultation to that of service provision. The following sections describe the varied tasks that community organizations undertake and the roles and actions of consultants who provide consultation, technical assistance, and service.

TASKS AND ACTIONS

Reaching Out to the Community

A primary task in strengthening organizations and community groups is to facilitate the involvement of the community of interest in the process (Chaskin, Brown, Venkantesh, and Vidal, 2001; Floyd et al., 2003; Kreztmann and McKnight, 1993; Kubisch et al., 2002; Rappaport, 1984, 1987; Solomon, 1976, 1987). It is important to collaborate with the community in defining who the stakeholders are and to ensure that these stakeholders represent the diversity of the community. Roles and responsibilities of the stakeholders, including consumers, are clarified as the process of change is planned and placed into action. Issues of cultural competence are critical to building bridges among diverse constituents in an effort to promote organizational and community change. When partnerships and collaboratives are effective, strategies for reaching out to the community have been successful. (Chapter 3 on cultural competence and chapter 4 on community collaborations give further discussion on the importance of outreach to communities.)

Building Leadership

Leadership is key to successful community building efforts (Chaskin et al., 2001; Floyd et al., 2003; Kretzmann and McKnight, 1993; Kubisch et al., 2002). Often the work of the consultant is to assist in the development of leadership skills. The development of these skills requires attention to the individual needs of each leader or developing leader or leadership team. Supporting leadership development can involve tasks as straightforward as helping a small organization develop an organizational structure that includes electing formal officers to assisting an organization in strengthening its relationship with its board of directors. In instances where new funding has significantly increased the staffing and operating budget of an organization, leadership development efforts may involve assisting with the development of formal personnel policies or training staff for diverse job roles and responsibilities. Within community partnerships, the role of the consultant often is to support the development of leadership in consumers and other community members. The items below denote strategies we have found to be helpful through our work with communities.

PROMOTING CONSUMER INVOLVEMENT AND LEADERSHIP

- Identify and acknowledge expertise of consumers
- Provide incentives and resources to enable consumers to actively participate (e.g., child care, flexible meeting times)
- Value and promote culturally competent interactions
- Provide opportunities for decision making (e.g., committee involvement)
- Encourage peer support and mutual assistance
- Offer leadership training opportunities

Developing a Plan for Action

Defining clearly what needs to be accomplished in the process of consultation, technical assistance, and service is a key task (e.g., Brown, 1995; Fetterman, 2001; Fetterman, Kaftarian, and Wandersman, 1996; Linney and Wandersman, 1991). While the process is most often determined by needs identified by the organization (i.e., client-identified needs), consultation, technical assistance, and service also occur in response to accountability or evaluative requirements of a funder (e.g., foundations or state or federal agencies). In any instance, it is imperative that the provider, the funder, and the community group or organization work together to define the expected outcomes of the support being provided. This plan should stress choosing strategies to build on *assets* and address *needs*. A process that is being used by many organizations to support a plan for action is a logic model (see Flerx's discussion in chapter 6). Logic models are used to enhance knowledge of what is working and guiding ongoing efforts for program improvement and program replication. The logic model may be specific to a project or program or it may be used to define the work of the consultant and the expected outcomes of the contractual period.

Obtaining Needed Resources

No matter how a community-building effort is established, resources are needed to keep the effort alive (e.g., Kretzmann and McKnight, 1993; Mattessich and Monsey, 1992; Rabin, 1992). Resources range from fiscal to material to human. Clearly, attention to resources is important to keeping the process of community building underway. Often community initiatives come into existence with grant funding. Such funding tends to be short-term (e.g., two to five years) and to decrease annually with an expectation that community replacement resources will increase annually. The work of such initiatives must extend beyond the initial funding period to make the needed changes or institutionalize the efforts.

Building Infrastructure

Whether a community effort is led by a small task force or by a well-funded organization, successful community-building efforts require attention to infrastructure issues (e.g., Andrews, Motes, Floyd, Flerx, and Lòpez-De Fede, 2005; Mitchell, Florin, and Stevenson, 2002). It is critical that there be strategies that support efficient and effective management of resources and assurance of quality of processes and products. Many of the current community-based interventions are centered on the implementation of evidence-based practices (Mitchell, Florin, and Stevenson, 2002; also see Flerx's discussion in chapter 6). Implicit in such practices is the adherence to the fidelity of the model, while implicit in community-building efforts is blending the fidelity of the model with the demands and resources of the community. The role of the consultant is to ensure the quality of this blending.

Vignette: Building Capacity Through Peer Support

Consultants and community developers promote organizational capacity building through peer support. Typically, they facilitate such support through interagency meetings and cross-site conferences where grantees that share a common funding source gather to focus on lessons learned about organizational development process and outcomes. Sometimes, their sharing leads to broader systems change. The following is an example:

A foundation awarded grants to several organizations in a metropolitan area that served the chronically unemployed. The organizations included a sheltered workshop for people with addictions, a culinary school that

(continued)

trained people for upscale food-service jobs, a church-based program for people who lived on the streets, a program that provided cars to family wage earners, and programs designed to develop job skills. Each was serving slightly different populations with common needs.

Prior to receiving funds from the foundation, the agencies had not had regular contact with one another. As part of the funded initiative, they met quarterly over a three-year period. They discussed successes, challenges, and results. Keeping a record of the themes of their discussions, they noticed a pattern had begun to emerge. They realized that each of them was part of a potential system. They sketched a flow chart that identified the systemwide steps of outreach, assessment, and intervention through the various specialties of their organizations, job placement, and follow-through. They facilitated efforts to get the foundation to fund formal development of such a peer support system that could enhance the work of all of their organizations and support sustainability of these efforts.

Measuring Success

In chapter 6 of this volume, Flerx focuses on the importance of evaluation through her discussion of building self-evaluation capacity within community organizations (e.g., Fetterman, 1994; Fetterman, Kaftarian, and Wandersman, 1996; Fetterman and Wandersman, 2004; Linney, and Wandersman, 1991; Whitmore, 1990). That chapter provides significant details on the importance of planning for success by developing program and evaluation plans from the start of the community-building effort.

Particularly, outcome evaluation relies on a common understanding of goals, measures of success, etc. However, as the following vignette illustrates, finding that common ground can be challenging at times.

Vignette: When Stakeholders Choose Conflicting Outcomes

Building a common understanding of programs and expectations for resources, consumers reached, and results are the basics that shape outcome evaluation. Defining the outcomes or program results, however, can be challenging. A

(continued)

recent scenario involving a clash of cultures between grassroots organizations and a philanthropic foundation illustrates this challenge.

Daniel, codirector of the Our Savior Church JOBS program, exudes energy and warmth. He spends much of each day recruiting young men and women who have dropped out of school, work, and home and are on the street, in jail, in shelters, or seeking emergency aid. His goal is to enroll them in the church's job-skills readiness program, a three-month, daily, semistructured experience that provides information, basic skills, connections to mentors, and inspiration to help the participants enter and stay in jobs or school. He has been known to sit for two hours on the doorstep of an apartment, waiting for a young man to appear so that he could develop a relationship with him. Out of about five hundred potential participants he talks to each year, about one hundred enroll, and forty complete the program. From Daniel's perspective, every person who has been reached has been offered hope and information. If they choose not to take advantage of the opportunity at the time he meets them or cannot because of challenges in their lives, he believes they are still better prepared to make the choice later.

The JOBS program received a grant from the area community foundation. Tim, a corporate lawyer who sits on the board of the foundation, takes his responsibility quite seriously as grant awards are decided. His hectic schedule limits the amount of time he has for meetings and site visits, but he is passionate about social justice and dedicated to helping his community develop. Tim is keenly aware that for every grant awarded, two other grant applications are denied. He looks for best practices and applies his business skills to assess each application as a potential investment that can yield quantifiable results in terms of lives changed and jobs acquired.

From Daniel's perspective, outcomes are matters of the heart. Touching even one person's life with knowledge about how to get reconnected with essential community support is a significant result. From Tim's perspective, outcomes are matters of stewardship, maximizing efficient use of resources to reach as many people as possible.

Promoting Sustainability

When community-building efforts are successful, sustaining these efforts is critical. For a technical assistance provider to this process, skills in disseminating the findings and in building on successes and lessons learned are essential.

Table 2.1 provides examples of the ways in which actions that support community capacity-building efforts (e.g., reaching out to community, building

TABLE 2.1: Consultation, Technical Assistance, Service: Examples of Supportive Actions

Tasks	Consultation	Technical Assistance	Service
Reaching out to community (e.g., Chaskin et al., 2001; Floyd et al., 2003; Kreztmann and McKnight, 1993; Kubisch et al., 2002)	Encourage the development of a workplace that reflects the diversity of the community served	Conduct cultural competency training with agency board of directors and administrators	Recruit and hire director of cultural-competency programs for agency
Building leadership (e.g., Chaskin et al., 2001; Floyd et al., 2003; Kreztmann and McKnight, 1993; Kubisch et al., 2002)	Recommend areas/topics to be considered in policies and procedures manual	Provide board training; facilitate development of policies and procedures	Develop policy and procedures manual for organization
Developing a plan for action (e.g., Brown, 1995; Fetterman, 2001; Fetterman, Kaftarian, and Wandersman, 1996; Linney and Wandersman, 1991)	Conduct needs and resource assessment; offer recommendations to program staff	Work with program staff to develop logic models based on needs and resources identified	Implement program plan for organization

TABLE 2.1: Consultation, Technical Assistance, Service: Examples of
Supportive Actions (*continued*)

Tasks	Consultation	Technical Assistance	Service
Obtaining needed resources (e.g., Kretzmann and McKnight, 1993; Rabin 1992; Mattessich and Monsey, 1992)	Review possible funding options available to community group	Provide training, resources, and review of efforts to respond to grant application; coach organization through grant-writing efforts	Write and submit grant application on behalf of organization
Building infrastructure (e.g., Mitchell, Florin, and Stevenson, 2002; Motes, Andrews, Floyd, Flerx, and Lòpez-De Fede, 2005)	Recommend needed components of an MIS plan to ensure accountability	Provide training to support the development of MIS system	Develop MIS system, input data, generate accountability reports
Measuring success (e.g., Fetterman, 1994; Fetterman, Kaftarian, and Wandersman, 1996; Fetterman and Wandersman, 2004; Linney and Wandersman, 1991; Whitmore, 1990)	Offer recommendations regarding the use of external evaluative process or internal (self-evaluation) process	Coach team in the development and implementation of self-evaluation of specific project.	Evaluate the progress of a specific project (e.g., collect data, analyze data, and issue evaluative report)
Promoting sustainability (e.g., Kreztmann and McKnight, 1993; Mattessich and Monsey, 1992)	Recommend that issues of sustainability need to be assessed and addressed.	Facilitate the development of a sustainability plan	Develop marketing literature and engage in lobbying efforts to support the continuation of the program

leadership) may vary based on the tasks of consultation, technical assistance, and service. This table is built on key principles within the field of community psychology, which place a strong emphasis on empowerment (e.g., Rappaport, 1984, 1987; Solomon, 1987).

COACHING: PROVIDING TECHNICAL ASSISTANCE AS CAPACITY-BUILDING CONSULTANTS

There probably are as many ways of providing technical assistance as there are technical assistance providers. However, one approach frequently described is coaching; this describes the primary strategy used by the contributors to this volume. According to Brown, Pitt, and Hirota (1999), "coaching" is an approach in which "support guidance, and encouragement [are offered] to key players in an initiative [that] helps them recognize and work through the fundamental tensions that must be negotiated as [an initiative] develops" (pp. 2–3), by building participants' capacities "to undertake the complex challenges of comprehensive service delivery and community building" (p. 7). Brown, Pitt, and Hirota posit four primary dimensions of a coach: (1) "carrying the vision of the initiative," (2) "fostering learning communities," (3) "facilitating dialogue and productive interaction among initiative participants," and (4) "developing capacity" (p. 7). Fetterman, Kaftarian, and Wandersman, (1996) offer the term "coach" in reference to empowerment evaluators who support others in conducting self-evaluation. Fetterman and colleagues describe coaching as a strategy that deliberately works to foster improvement and self-determination. Coaches are attentive to empowering processes and outcomes, where the coach and the individuals benefiting from the coaching, are able to learn from each other.

The extent of a coach's engagement with an agency, organization, or community group depends on a variety of factors. Size, type (e.g., private, nonprofit, state government), history, and venue influence the relationship between the organization and the coach that will emerge over time. It is essential that the coach be ever mindful that the process and the outcomes belong to the organization or group. The community members also may need to be reminded of their ownership from time to time. A common danger is for the coach to become the leader and take responsibility for the success or the failure of an organization's endeavors.

Even in the more receptive settings, a capacity-building consultant must be prepared to confront various obstacles, including resistance, interference, delays, and criticism. It is unrealistic to expect unanimous acceptance of any proposed change. Even in organizations or groups where there is broad support for revising ways of doing things, there may be least one person who will not agree with a decision or approach. Overt or covert attempts to interfere with the coach's work with the organization or with the organization's own efforts to bring about change can occur. Delays from internal or external sources can interfere with change efforts. All of these obstacles come with the territory, and the wise coach will anticipate them and have a plan for handling them.

Technical assistance is a planned intervention to facilitate change. Community groups and organizations may seek technical assistance to bring about changes in service delivery systems, programs, information systems, and even political agendas. These interventions call for a blend of practice-wisdom and social science, and the different perspectives and experiences of practitioners and coaches can interact to produce innovations that neither could bring about alone. Practitioners will have an understanding of the unique characteristics of the individuals that an intervention is intended to help, as well as the environments in which the intervention will be integrated. The coaches will bring theoretical and applied methods for accomplishing the predicted outcomes. Coaches work closely with practitioners to assure that the intervention methods incorporate these various understandings in a way that will achieve desired results. It is the blend of theoretical and practical knowledge that maximizes the success or effectiveness of a program.

THE THEORETICAL BASES FOR PROVIDING TECHNICAL ASSISTANCE

Three sets of theories support and clarify issues related to technical assistance offered to organizations and communities: empowerment theory, organizational change theory; and adult learning theory. These theories intersect to guide professionals who offer technical assistance, helping them identify the desired outcome of change and empowerment; understand the conditions in which change can occur; and focus on the primary method through which technical assistance is delivered and received—adult learning.

Empowerment Theory

Empowerment is a core concept in the fields of social work (e.g., Lee, 1994, 2001; Solomon, 1976, 1987) and community psychology (e.g., Rappaport, 1984, 1987) and offers direction for change at individual, small group, organization, and community levels. Solomon (1987) refers to empowerment as the "reduction of an overriding sense of powerlessness to direct one's own life in the direction of reasonable personal gratification" (p. 80). With an emphasis on social justice, Solomon (1976) originally coined the term "empowerment" to describe the actions of disenfranchised African Americans in becoming a significant force in shaping political ideology and resources. The stigmatized collective experiences of African Americans served as the backdrop for the importance given to the empowerment approach in helping individuals perceive themselves as competent individuals able to "gain control over the forces" (Solomon, 1987, p. 81) that determine the quality of life. Similarly, Lee (1994, 2001) provides examples of group empowerment work, political activities, and individual- and family-oriented empowerment practice through her work with diverse disenfranchised groups (e.g., the homeless, the mentally ill, and victims of abuse and neglect.)

Rappaport (1984, 1987) defines empowerment within the community psychology literature as a process by which people, organizations, and communities gain control over issues of importance to them. Recent discourse on empowerment (Peterson, Hamme, and Speer, 2002) highlights its emotional, cognitive, and behavioral aspects. Emotional empowerment is described as relating to a sense of control over one's life and perceived competence to effect change. The cognitive component focuses on having a "critical understanding of the sociopolitical forces shaping the distribution of power and resources in the environment" (p. 338). And the behavioral component focuses on participatory action.

Empowerment theory recognizes that the creative, innovative, and productive capacities of people can be tapped more effectively if they participate in the activities that influence their lives (e.g., join in making decisions that directly affect them). Although the goal is self-determination and autonomy, empowerment also helps individuals, families, and groups develop methods and resources for engaging in interdependent relationships (Zimmerman, 2000).

Empowering processes help individuals, families, and communities gain control over decisions that affect them, obtain needed resources, and understand their social environments. It is a process by which people or organizations gain mastery over issues of concern to them (Rappaport, 1987; Solomon, 1976; Zimmerman, 2000). A process is considered empowering if it helps people develop problem-solving and decision-making skills. At the individual level, an empowering process may involve family participation in community organizations and groups; at the organizational level, it might include shared leadership and decision making; and at the community level, empowering processes might include accessible government, media, and other community resources (Zimmerman, 2000). Empowered people and communities have the necessary skills and resources to take control of their own lives.

Organizational Change Theory

The seminal work of Kurt Lewin (1951) has shaped our approach to change, and thus our change theory for technical assistance. Lewin proposed a "force field" analysis model to understand organizational change. Force field analysis is based on the proposition that an organization is typically in a state of equilibrium and that in order for change to occur there must be "driving forces" strong enough to establish the necessary conditions for change. We have found this model useful as an organizing framework to guide and facilitate community and organizational change through the coaching/technical assistance process. Building on the premises of Lewin's model, our approach to change theory considers six conditions that "drive" change within the technical assistance process: (1) an assessment of current and potential realities, (2) knowledge about how to make desired changes, (3) skills needed to make a change, (4) motivation or readiness to change, (5) opportunity to change, and (6) reinforcement of and support for making the change.

Current and potential realities include the community's sociopolitical climate, economic stability, and infrastructure for public services, such as education, transportation, and health care. On a more personal level, the history and psychosocial dynamic among political leaders, service agencies, and constituents must be considered.

How to go about facilitating change is not common knowledge. If it were, individuals, groups, and communities would not seek help from professional change agents. Too often, however, the change agent is seen as the *impetus* for the change rather than as the *facilitator* of change. One of the best inputs a capacity-building consultant can offer to a change effort is teaching the individuals who are involved with the process how to bring about that change and sustain it. The impact of these lessons is exponential because the learners can use the skills to effect change in other contexts. Teaching and modeling, then, are critical strategies for empowering individuals, families, and communities.

Change-making skills follow on the heels of change-making knowledge. Skill development and exchange represent important steps in achieving desired goals. Developing skills is, in fact, essential to using knowledge effectively. It is in the actual *doing* that people become comfortable with and competent in the change process. It is, in colloquial terms, "where the rubber meets the road." Through the partnering experience, stakeholders and the capacity-building consultant exchange aspects of their sets of skills. This exchange is another component of empowerment.

Unfortunately, knowledge and skills to bring about change are not sufficient qualities for change to happen. Change requires motivation or readiness on the part of the stakeholders. Motivation is an attitude that feeds people's energy and tolerance for the stress associated with change and its consequences (e.g., Maslow, 1943; Prochaska, Norcross, and DiClemente, 1994; Weiner, 1986). It is unlikely that a coach actually can motivate others to change. Part of the coach's task, however, is to assess motivation levels of those who will be involved in the change process as change agents and as intended and unintended beneficiaries. These readiness assessments should be regular and frequent, especially if there is a high level of resistance to change by major stakeholders. The task of the consultant is to identify the threats to motivation then to help stakeholders confront and resolve those threats.

Knowing when, where, and how the opportunity for change presents itself is important to the success of the change effort. Although the coach can bring an objective eye and ear to the potential opportunities, it is most likely that the stakeholders and constituents will have the best sense of when change is propitious.

One of the most critical roles the coach can play in working with communities is in reinforcing and supporting the change process. The consultant's objectivity offers some insulation to the frustrations that accompany efforts to bring about change (Beer and Walton, 1987). By monitoring progress and helping indigenous change agents stay conscious of their accomplishments, the coach can reduce the discouragement that can plague an effort to make changes in a community.

CONDITIONS FOR CHANGE. Individuals and communities typically seek change when they are confronted with events or experiences that challenge their well-being. When readiness to change reaches a critical level, efforts to obtain knowledge and skills to make a change are initiated. As these elements increase, opportunities for actually undertaking change are acted upon or created. For effective change to occur and stabilize, there must be ecological support and reinforcement: for example, economic investments, political backing, or broad-based, grassroots endorsement.

Consultants generally begin working with individuals or community groups after they realize the need for change; usually an initial consultation consists of advice on methods or strategies for assessing the community and its needs, resources, and strengths. The findings of this assessment form the basis of a technical assistance plan to help the community acquire the knowledge and skills needed to implement its desired or chosen change. The synergy of multiple perspectives increases the likelihood that opportunities for change will be identified and engaged. Finally, celebrating the progress community groups make in achieving their goals is an important part of providing technical assistance.

Adult Learning Theory

There is not "one" adult learning theory, but rather as Merriam (2001) explains "a mosaic of theories, models, sets of principles, and explanations that, combined, compose the knowledge base of adult learning" (p. 3). However, much of what is understood about adult learning is built upon the work of Knowles (1975, 1984a, 1984b) who first introduced the concept of andragogy, the art and science of adult learning. Over time, however, this concept has taken on a broader meaning (Conner, 2004). Rather than a distinct form of learning from pedagogy (as is the case with child or preadult learning), Conner points out that andragogy currently stresses learner-focused approaches, not teacher-focused approaches. Thus the underlying assumptions of the andragogic model apply more generally to instructional activities with people of any age that are learner-centered, rather than specifically to adult learning.

The andragogic model is relevant to the coaching process. The model encourages (1) letting learners know why something is important to learn, (2) showing learners how to direct themselves through information, and (3) relating the topic to the learners' experiences. Additionally the model points out that (4) learning will not occur until the individual is ready and motivated to learn. Facilitating this readiness and motivation often requires (5) helping the learner to overcome inhibitions, behaviors, and beliefs about learning (Conner, 2004).

Adult learning theories posit that adults seek out learning experiences that will help them negotiate anticipated or experienced life-changing events (Knowles, Holton, and Swanson, 1998; Lavin and Dirkx, 1995; Zemke and Zemke, 1984) and that adult learning is influenced not only by chronological age but significantly by culture, ethnicity, personality, and political ethos (Brookfield, 1995). Adult learners are characterized as independent and self-directed learners who possess a wealth of life experience and knowledge. Most adult learners are goal oriented and seek practical, relevant learning experiences that will help them meet their personal and occupational goals. Most importantly, adults must be respected as they invest and engage in the learning process (Knowles, Holton, and Swanson, 1998).

The technical assistant's role in learning environments in which organizational staff at all levels, community leaders, and consumers participate is to facilitate experiential learning. Generally, this requires establishing a positive climate for learning, clarifying the purposes, organizing and offering learning resources, balancing the intellectual and emotional components of learning, and providing opportunities for both the adult students and the adult teacher to share reactions, thoughts, and feelings with each other (Rogers, 1961).

Chavis, Florin, and Felix (1993) point to the importance of social learning theory and adult learning theory in building strategies to support community organizations and groups. They describe the need to "be problem oriented, with experiential learning based on simulations and actual real life-experiences; be directed by the learner and his/her needs; allow for different learning styles; be sustained and readily accessible as questions and barriers emerge; use role modeling and peer learning (learning from people like oneself); be proactive; offer on-going support to participants; use multiple, mutually reinforcing methods; provide incentives for participation; and promote the adoption of new ideas" (pp. 47–48). These strategies, like the principles presented below, serve as important resources and guides to coaches who, in providing technical assistance, are facilitating a learning process.

PROVIDING TECHNICAL ASSISTANCE: KNOWLEDGE, SKILLS, VALUES AND ATTITUDES, AND QUALITIES

While the provision of technical assistance may not be explicitly discussed in the standards of practice of professions and professional organizations, they are clearly embedded within standards and ethics of practice. To illustrate, a recent publication by the American Evaluation Association (Fitzpatrick and Morris, 1999) draws attention to the need to be vigilant to ethics and standards of practice as professionals move into the many changing roles of supporters to community change. The following set of principles reflects our standards of practice and qualities for providing effective technical assistance to community groups.

Knowledge

Consultants providing technical assistance should have or obtain a solid understanding about their contractors' organization and community. This understanding is critical to providing effective technical assistance. Failure to learn fully about the community, including its social, economic, and political environments, resources, strengths, and needs, can result in blunders that not only can impede change but also can damage fragile relationships among stakeholders.

Coaches must also have a good grasp of various organizational and community development theories and validating research. It can be argued that professional ethics demand that advice be more than the professional's opinion and that empirical research should support that advice. Even the coach who is well grounded in change theory and research, with a solid understanding of the community and its stakeholders, is unlikely to be effective if he or she does not understand group process and dynamics. It is important to remember that when providing technical assistance, the coach's role is not to do the work of the community's members but to help them plan, organize, and implement interventions for the achievement of their goals.

Skills

Contractors' expectations of capacity-building consultants are varied and broad; therefore, coaches must possess a wide range of skills and competencies. It is not realistic, however, to expect each and every consultant to have all the skills desired by a contractor; that is why a team approach can be an effective method of providing technical assistance. Blending skills on a team maximizes the strengths and reduces the deficiencies that any one professional brings to the project. Another benefit of the team model is that community members can observe and participate in team-based activities and transfer those experiences to other collaborative opportunities. The technical assistance team, in partnership with the contractor and constituents, can create a synergy that maximizes the intervention efforts.

In our work with communities, we have found certain skills to be essential to successful coaching. These include skills in communication, programming (e.g., prevention and intervention), problem solving, and research. A coach who effectively communicates with contractors and constituents is able to relate to people across socioeconomic lines. Coaches must be able to connect with all stakeholders involved in the project. Sometimes the best way to communicate and connect is one-on-one, face-to-face, up close and personal. Other times, the best communication may be through traditional written means, such as letters and reports, the recommended method when a record of the communication might be important. Then, of course, a coach must have access to and a facility with technology to support ongoing communication (e.g., e-mail, Web services, teleconferencing). A coach who is not available regularly and consistently is of little use to a project.

Programming skills include planning, development, and implementation. The coach's role in programming is to help the contractor design an environment in which the partners can perform effectively to achieve their goals. When providing technical assistance for programming, the coach is a facilitator. It is important for the coach to remember that the program belongs to the contractor and, more importantly, to the constituents or the families the program is intended to serve. When the coach leaves the project, if the program is to continue, it must do so under the leadership and direction of others. The ultimate goal of the technical assistance is to build community capacity.

A coach can be particularly helpful to projects in problem solving. The consultant's objectivity and detachment are assets here because he or she is not, or should not be, affiliated with any community faction and does not have history with the stakeholders that would demand allegiance to an ideology or outcome. An effective consultant engaged in problem solving can assess a conflictual situation with an objective eye, one that sees the numerous facets of the conflict as well as multiple alternatives for resolving the conflict. Because stakeholders tend to be attached to their positions, often it is difficult for them to imagine or fully consider other options. Helping stakeholders find novel solutions to their conflicts requires skills in negotiation and mediation. There are numerous good resources for developing these skills; two recommended classics are *The Art of Negotiating* (Nierenberg, 1985) and *Getting to Yes: Negotiating Agreement Without Giving In* (Fisher, Ury, and Patton, 1991). Working with stakeholders to resolve conflicts and problems can be a very satisfying role for a coach if done with patience, empathy, and respect.

A cluster of important skill sets includes needs and resource assessment, building community collaboratives, and program evaluation. The area of program evaluation is one that can be intimidating for both the stakeholders and the coach. Later chapters in this book discuss various issues related to these skills and how to deal with them.

Values

While a coach may bring an objective approach to this work, consultation is not value-free. Every coach brings a value set to the consultation milieu. Contractors also have a value set that impinges on the consultant's work. When these values are in conflict and cannot be successfully mediated, the consultant should consider not accepting a contract. We have found in our work that there are fundamental values that promote the provision of effective technical assistance to build capacity that strengthens families, organizations, and communities. These values include a commitment to stakeholders' self-determination, the democratic process, and cultural competence.

Valuing self-determination embraces the prerogative of stakeholders to decide for themselves what course to take and the responsibility of stakeholders to account for the results and consequences of their choices (cf. Fetterman, 2001). Technical assistance coaches must guard against a paternalistic stance in which they attempt to impose a preferred strategy or program on the stakeholders (Simon, 1994). A commitment to self-determination requires TA coaches to walk a path between overinvolvement and detachment. When working with active groups, the threat is being too detached; with passive or lethargic groups, the danger is in becoming overly involved and too directive. Simon (1994) offers guidance to prevent paternalism through the periodic and conscientious use of self-inventory that focuses on key empowerment principles, such as attentiveness to implicit and explicit communications, openness to diverse opinions and alternative proposals, receptiveness to personal feedback (e.g., style, approach), and alertness to strengths and creativity. Ongoing self-examination helps coaches better facilitate the self-determination of program managers, evaluation teams, consumers, and other community partners.

Related to self-determination is our belief in the democratic process (Fetterman, 2001) that includes providing opportunities for all stakeholder voices to be heard and incorporated into a program or system. It does not mean that there must be a vote on every issue. There are many issues that can be addressed by one individual or a small group of individuals. The thrust of the democratic process is that the people who are part of the program or system, including all levels of service providers and their clients, are offered genuine opportunities for participating in the planning, development, implementation, and evaluation of the program or system with which they are involved.

Cultural competence is essential to working with community groups. Chapter 3 in this book deals with the challenges of supporting organizations in becoming more culturally competent.

Attitude

Attitudes are closely aligned with values, but they deserve a separate discussion because stakeholders encounter a consultant's attitudes before they are conscious of the consultant's values. Self-determination is linked to a strengths perspective, that is, a focus on the strengths of families, organizations, and communities. When we are called in to provide technical assistance, we usually are presented with a problem that needs to be addressed. This can set up an approach that focuses on the weaknesses of the community or some part of it. The challenge is to identify and build on or encompass sectors in the community that are already strong and functioning well. Our task is to build upon the existing strengths and competencies.

Two other important and related attitudes are genuine respect for others and humility. These attitudes emerge as behavioral by-products of our skills and values. However, our educational backgrounds and our expert status can betray us if we are not aware of their effects on the people with and for whom we work. Arrogance has no legitimate place in the consultant's repertoire.

Qualities

Consultants providing technical assistance may have many personal and professional qualities and characteristics. We have found that there are four necessary qualities and characteristics that cut across almost all projects: expertise, autonomy, enabling and facilitating, and conscientiousness.

EXPERTISE. A conventional definition—the hallmark—of a technical assistance coach is an expert in some area who has knowledge or skills that someone else needs. A coach providing technical assistance is the expert at the *beginning* of the work he or she is employed to do for the contractor. It is *not* on-the-job training. Coaches not only promote their expertise, but they also must admit their deficiencies or inadequacies. Being called into a community as a capacity-building consultant can be a heady experience, but the coach must be careful not to promise more than can be delivered. An honest appraisal of oneself to oneself and then to the contractors can help avoid embarrassing or litigious consequences.

AUTONOMY. To maintain objectivity toward the project and its participants, the consultant offering technical assistance must see himself or herself and be seen by the project's participants as autonomous and independent. This stance reinforces the trust that the participants need in the consultant and in their mutual communications.

ENABLING AND FACILITATING. Whether initiated by funding requirements or by leaders of community projects, the primary purpose of technical assistance is to help the community group or organization achieve desired goals. It is rare, if ever, that a community group wants a capacity-building consultant to impose his or her solutions on the group. Rather, the coach is expected to enable and facilitate the group in meeting its goals—through, by, and for the group. This requires supportive, not directive, qualities. The risk of crossing these boundaries and becoming directive is particularly acute when the consultant is providing technical assistance because stakeholders often are hesitant or reluctant to forge ahead with making or implementing decisions. However, the prudent consultant will resist pressure to drive the project to its conclusion.

CONSCIENTIOUSNESS. Sometimes, having the diligence to carry through with one's commitments and responsibilities can be a problem for consultants. This particularly is true when the consultant is providing technical assistance to an organization that has minimal or no skills in the area for which the consultant is engaged. Sometimes the coach's patience and energy are dissipated because the project may seem to drag on at a very slow pace or face time-consuming obstacles. It is important for the contractor and the coach to specify in the beginning what tasks will be assigned to whom, how interruptions or hurdles will be handled, when final decisions will be made and by whom, and a timetable not only for project completion but also for periodic evaluation of the project's goals and the feasibility of accomplishing them. In addition, a clear threat to the consultant's conscientiousness is ambiguity about his or her role or responsibilities.

The following case example illustrates challenges that may be faced when providing technical assistance.

Vignette: Sometimes Capacity Isn't Built: An Example Highlighting the Importance of Assessing Readiness and Maintaining Contractual Roles

As capacity-building consultants, we provided technical assistance in the area of evaluation to a statewide after-school program sponsored by a state office of Communities in Schools. We approached the work with CIS with a goal of building capacity for self-evaluation by staff of local programs funded by the state office. Our team coached the local programs in the implementation of the project design and the evaluation plan. Because the

(continued)

goals were determined statewide, there were some common outcome indicators such as grades, standardized test scores, attendance, and discipline. The funder, in consultation with the technical assistance team, proposed to assess the impact of the statewide programs on the self-concept of the students served. While there were multiple strategies across the numerous sites, both the coaches and CIS felt that the research literature supported that the overall activities (whatever the variance) could result in an improved sense of self.

The coaching team selected an assessment instrument to measure students' self-concept at the beginning and end of the school year. The instrument was selected because it provided a multidimensional measure of self-concept that matched many of the goals of the after-school program. The information from the assessment measure could assist case managers in providing services to students. The results could be used to track changes in students' overall self-concept and level of self-esteem. Further, the assessment scores could be used to better understand students' relationships toward teachers and their feelings toward their academic performance. Finally, the scale assessed student satisfaction with their current friendships.

The practical reasons for selecting the particular assessment measure included the suggested age range for use; the length of administration; the administration format; content and construct validity; the test-retest reliability; and the standardization of the measure, which included African American, low-income, and rural populations.

After selecting the assessment instrument, the coaches met with their liaison, the director of evaluation for CIS, to discuss the proposed use of the scale with the after-school programs. At this time, the coaching team provided the liaison with a handout that summarized the measure and how it addressed the primary goals of the program and its ability to support the case-management aspect of the after-school programs. Our liaison endorsed the instrument and presented it to the executive directors of the local after school programs at a program planning retreat.

The liaison returned from the retreat with much excitement. Not only were the executive directors in agreement with the decision to use this measure, they were excited about its ability to support individual planning for the case management aspects of their programs. In fact, the executive

(continued)

directors insisted that they needed the data as soon as possible in order to support their work with individual students and to assist them in considering options to support overall program development.

We were pleased with this response and viewed it as evidence that our coaching was actually building evaluation capacity. Executive directors, who at other times had resisted using a ten-item survey to gather data about program objectives, were now agreeing to use a standardized instrument with seventy-two items. They wanted the data in a timely fashion. They wanted to use the data to shape the work of their programs. This was reinforcement that our coaching was making a difference.

We wanted to honor the requests of the sites for timely feedback and to support the immediate use of the data for program improvement. In order to achieve this feat, our team was asked to facilitate the administration, scoring, and reporting of findings for more than 3,000 students within a six-week time frame. We hired temporary staff and literally worked nonstop over this period to get these data back to program sites. We met the deadline.

We prepared a presentation for an upcoming meeting of executive directors on how to use the data from the assessment measure. The presentation summarized how to read the individual profile sheets as well as how to use the data for individual case-management planning and to support overall program development. During our presentation, the executive directors asked many questions related to technical issues about the instrument, while other questions focused on general use of the data. Many expressed concern that the data for individual students might require high levels of clinical skill to adequately support student needs (most program staff members are trained at the bachelor's level). For example, executive directors felt that the profile sheets were complex and would require significant time and clinical skill to review and make determinations about how to use these data with students and their families. They raised concerns regarding the complexity of using the results of the scale to determine the appropriate delivery of case-management services.

In general, the executive directors expressed their feelings that the data and information presented were very helpful but much more clinically in-depth than they felt prepared to handle. Many feared that the individual

(*continued*)

findings might make them liable for the clinical outcomes of their students. While comfortable with more general after-school activities and interventions, the presentation of the data caused the executive directors to question the capacity of their programs to provide individual case-management services. The executive directors, with support of the funder, decided to embargo the data. It would not be used at any program site until a task force could be convened to review this further and offer recommendations to the funder. The task force met and decided that individual program sites would not be required to use the assessment data from the initial assessments nor be required to administer the post-assessments. The task force recommended that using the data for case-management and program development purposes was optional. In fact, only one program site decided to use the data.

As coaches, we were unprepared for this response. We had worked non-stop for six weeks to accomplish the task of giving them the data as they had requested. We had met an extremely tight deadline. While the executive directors had initially expressed excitement over using this instrument to support the after-school programs, now that the data were available to them, they didn't want to use it.

We were very comfortable with the appropriateness of the assessment measure for the students. We also were very confident that the CIS liaison had adequately presented the information that described the measure to the executive directors. We were further confident that his feedback to us was accurate. In fact, we received inquiries from some executive directors who wanted to know when the data would be available to them.

So what went wrong? After debriefing sessions within our team, with our CIS liaison, and with other colleagues, we are able to offer some reflections on what happened. We realized that our excitement about program staff connecting the value of assessment data in relationship to program implementation had overshadowed our own good practices as coaches. We focused so much on the "success" of the executive directors in getting this valuable connection that *we neglected to provide the essential support necessary for success. We also overstepped our contractual roles and took on service roles.* We spent so much time getting the "data" that we were unable to provide the needed technical assistance to ensure that the data would

(*continued*)

benefit the local programs. *We neglected to assess the "readiness"* for using the assessment data.

Contrary to our usual coaching practices, we did not assess the readiness of programs to understand these data, use these data, or benefit programmatically from these data. In working to build community capacity, our typical practice is to conduct early assessments of readiness for new strategies, for new approaches, for readiness for change. These readiness data shape our intervention strategies, making them unique to each program. Assessing program readiness would have allowed our teams to tailor the coaching to the needs of the particular programs and would have supported the programs to successfully use the self concept data in benefiting the after school programs.

As a technical assistance team, we could have supported readiness assessment through varied coaching strategies. For example:

1. As coaches we work very closely with program sites and had developed trusting relationships and open communications with these sites. As a follow-up to the executive directors' retreat, we could have provided technical assistance to the executive directors and program staff to further explain this instrument. These explanations would have allowed us to discuss the instrument in greater detail, clarify expectations, and really get *informed acceptance of* the use of the instrument. Sites vary in the level of commitment and readiness to engage in new approaches and strategies. Technical assistance at the local program level would have allowed for better discernment of how well this instrument could be used within each site.

2. While we did a thorough job researching self-concept measures to select an appropriate instrument for this population, we spent little time *determining the best strategy* for helping sites learn how to use the data. We focused on the beginning (providing the needed service to collect the initial assessment data) but not the "end." As coaches, we might have drafted mock profile sheets and provided examples to program staff on how to use the data to support individual case-management planning (e.g., when to make a referral to a mental health professional) as well as broader program goals and objectives (e.g., establishing parenting programs that focus on effective discipline). Executive directors first saw profile sheets and were instructed on how to interpret them after the data were collected.

(continued)

They did not have time to implement appropriate programmatic supports. The depth of the information received from the assessment measure was unimaginable to the executive directors, and they became overwhelmed by receiving the information after the data had been collected. The time between selection of a measurement tool and the presentation of the results was spent "getting to the data." Because we had not contracted to provide the service of data collection, we did not have the needed time to prepare the program staff to effectively use the data.

3. Individual case-management planning for each child was a newly established requirement for the after-school sites. We learned that program staff ranged in case-management abilities from those uncomfortable conducting intake interviews with students to others with good training and years of experience in counseling youth. Many without significant case-management skills could be excited about new learning; others could be fearful of liabilities and responsibilities. Assessing readiness by *focusing on knowledge, skills, and attitudes* associated with case management would have allowed the coaches to better support the particular needs of program sites. Prior assessment of case-management approaches and strategies would have further allowed our team, CIS state office staff, and local executive directors to better determine the match between this self-concept measure and the program implementation requirements.

In the excitement of seeing increased levels of capacity for evaluation being built, we lost sight of our own good practices related to coaching. Assessing readiness is the essential first step to building evaluation capacity. Further, assessing readiness requires attention to contractual roles and responsibilities that support the capacity-building work.

CONCLUSIONS

The provision of consultation, technical assistance, and outsourced services are integral to the growing movement toward building organizational and community capacity. However, being attentive to the differences among these roles is important. This chapter has primarily focused on consultants who provide technical assistance, especially capacity-building consultants or coaches.

Funding entities, especially foundations, are requiring grantees to demonstrate that their investments are being well used and are benefiting the intended constituencies. Meeting such requirements requires knowledge and skills that many community-based organizations and groups do not readily possess. Technical assistance provides an opportunity to support the goals of diverse funders and the needs of the recipients of these funds.

While there is significant market demand for technical assistance, this chapter points out the pitfalls and possibilities of providing technical assistance. The consultant must negotiate a contractual relationship that spells out the roles of the consultant, distinguishing clearly among consultation, technical assistance, and service. Success with this one task will avoid a multitude of problems that can impinge on the success of the community-building efforts. While knowledge, skills, and theory/research-based action are clearly imperative to providing effective technical assistance, attending to ethical standards is equally important. As diverse professionals allow technical assistance to assume larger roles, standards are emerging. Whether one is engaging in technical assistance to help an organization clarify its mission, implement evidence-based practices, build coalitions, or facilitate self-evaluation, it is imperative to be vigilant about the ethics of one's work. Because grants and other funding resources are clearly the impetus of much of the current technical assistance requests, issues such as motivation for change or community readiness for change must be assessed to determine how effective one can be in the role of technical assistant for community change. Such assessments can delineate the technical assistance context, thus aiding the funder, the community program, and the consultant in establishing realistic capacity-building goals. Further, the reader is encouraged to remember that technical assistance requires much patience, reflection, and humility in the doing and in the evaluating.

As consultants to a wide array of community-building processes, professionals benefit from numerous possibilities, including being a partner in capacity building, seeing community change, and effecting meaningful outcomes. For academics and researchers, the medium of technical assistance provides an outstanding opportunity to bridge research and practice. Whatever their auspices, those providing technical assistance benefit from sharing experiences with others, which expands our knowledge, refines our skills, and releases our creativity.

References

Andrews, A. B., Motes, P. S., Floyd, A. G., Flerx, V. C., and Lòpez–De Fede, A. (2005). Building evaluation capacity in community-based organizations: Reflections of an empowerment evaluation team. *Journal of Community Practice, 13* (4).

Aspen Institute. (2002). *Voices from the field: Learning from the early work of CCIs.* Washington, D.C.: Aspen Institute.

Beer, M., and Walton, A. E. (1987). Organization change and development. *Annual Review of Psychology, 38*, 339–67.

Block, P. (1981). *Flawless consulting: A guide to getting your experience used.* San Diego: Pfieffer and Company.

Brookfield, S. (1995). Adult learning: An overview. In A. Tuinjman (Ed.), *International encyclopedia of education.* Oxford: Pergamon Press.

Brown, P. (1995). The role of the evaluator in comprehensive community initiatives. In J. P. Connell, A. C. Kubisch, L. B. Schorr, and C. H. Weiss (Eds.) *New approaches to evaluating community initiatives: Concepts, methods, and contexts* (pp. 201–25). Washington, D.C.: Aspen Institute.

Brown, P., Pitt, J., and Hirota, J. (1999). *New approaches to technical assistance: The role of the coach.* Chicago: Chapin Hall.

Bruner, C. (1993). *So you think you need some help? Making effective use of technical assistance.* New York: National Center for Integration Clearinghouse, National Center for Children in Poverty: Columbia University.

Chaskin, R. J., Brown, P., Venkatesh, S., and Vidal, A. (2001). *Building community capacity.* New York: Aldine de Gruyter.

Chavis, D. M., Florin, P., and Felix, M. R. J. (1993). Nurturing grassroots initiatives for community development: The role of enabling systems. In T. Mizrahi and J. Morrison (Eds.), *Community and social administration: Advances, trends, and emerging principles* (pp. 41–63). New York: Haworth Press.

Conner, M. L. (2004). How adults learn. *Ageless Learner, 1997–2004.* Retrieved January 10, 2005, from http://agelesslearner.com/intros/adultlearning.html.

Fetterman, D. (1994). Empowerment evaluation. *Evaluation Practice, 15* (1), 1–15.

Fetterman, D. (2001). Empowerment evaluation and self-determination: A practical approach toward program improvement and capacity building. In N. Schneiderman and M. A. Speers (Eds.), *Integrating behavioral and social sciences with public health* (pp. 321–50). Washington, D.C.: American Psychological Association.

Fetterman, D., Kaftarian, S., and Wandersman, A. (Eds.). (1996). *Empowerment evaluation: Knowledge and tools for self-assessment and accountability.* Thousand Oaks, Calif.: Sage.

Fetterman, D. M., and Wandersman, A. (Eds.). (2004). *Empowerment evaluation principles in practice.* New York: Guilford Publications

Fisher, R., Ury, W., and Patton, B. (1991). *Getting to yes: Negotiating agreement without giving in* (2nd ed.). New York: Penguin.

Fitzpatrick, J. L., and Morris, M. (1999). *New directions for evaluation: Current and emerging ethical challenges in evaluation* (No. 82). San Francisco: Jossey-Bass.

Floyd, A. G., Andrews, A. B., Hess, P., Flerx, V. C., Rivers, J., Phillips, L., Whiting, J. A., Malson, M. R., and Kinnard, D. (2003). *Lessons learned and affirmed: The Duke Endowment Children and Families Program, final report*. Columbia, S.C.: University of South Carolina, Institute for Families in Society.

Knowles, M. S. (1975). *Self-directed learning*. Chicago: Follet.

Knowles, M. S. (1984a). *The adult learner: A neglected species* (3rd ed.). Houston, Tex.: Gulf Publishing.

Knowles, M. S. (1984b). *Andragogy in action*. San Francisco: Jossey-Bass.

Knowles, M. S., Holton, E. F., Swanson, R.A. (1998). *The adult learner* (5th ed.). Woburn, Mass.: Butterworth-Heinemann.

Kretzmann, J. P., and McKnight, J. L. (1993). *Building communities from the inside out: A path toward finding and mobilizing a community's assets*. Chicago: ACTA Publications.

Kubisch, A. C., Auspos, P., Brown, P., Chaskin, R., Fulbright-Anderson, K., and Hamilton, R. (2002). *Voices from the field II: Reflections on comprehensive community change*. Washington, D.C.: Aspen Institute.

Lavin, R. S., and Dirkx, J. M. (1995). Teacher beliefs about staff development via distance learning: A research approach in planning practice. In R. Orem and C. Mealman (Eds.), *Proceedings of the fourteenth Midwest research-to-practice conference in adult, continuing, and community education* (pp. 125–30). DeKalb: Northern Illinois University and National Louis University.

Lee, J. (1994). *The empowerment approach to social work practice*. New York: Columbia University Press.

Lee, J. (2001). *The empowerment approach to social work practice* (2nd ed.). New York: Columbia University Press.

Lewin, K. (1951). *Field theory in social science; selected theoretical papers*. New York: Harper and Row.

Linney, J. A., and Wandersman, A. (Eds.). (1991). *Prevention plus III: Assessing alcohol and other drug prevention programs at the school and community level: A four step guide to useful program assessment*. Rockville, Md.: Office for Substance Abuse Prevention.

Maslow, A. (1943). A theory of motivation. *Journal of Applied Psychology, 12* (4), 441–80.

Mattessich, P. W., and Monsey, B. R. (1992). *Collaboration: What makes it work*. St. Paul, Minn.: Amherst H. Wilder Foundation.

Merriam, S. B. (2001). *The new update on adult learning theory*. San Francisco: Jossey-Bass.

Mitchell, R. E., Florin, P., and Stevenson, J. F. (2002). Supporting community-based prevention and health promotion initiatives: Developing effective technical assistance systems. *Health Education and Behavior, 29* (5), 620–39.

Moorhouse, D. R. (2002). Evaluation results of the 2002 user satisfaction survey. Nova Southeastern University: University Research and Planning. Retrieved February 22, 2005, from http://www.nova.edu/rpga/reports/forms/2002/02-13f.pdf.

Networks for Training and Development, Inc. (n.d.). Home page. Retrieved February 22, 2005, from http://networksfortraining.org/consult04.htm.

Nierenberg, G. I. (1985). *The art of negotiating.* New York: E. F. Dutton.

Peterson, N. A., Hamme, C. L., and Speer, P. W. (2002). Interactional empowerment of African Americans and Caucasians: Differences in understandings of power, political functioning, and shaping ideology. *Journal of Black Studies, 32* (3), 336–51.

Prochaska, J., Norcross, J., and DiClemente, C. (1994). *Changing for good.* New York: Avon Books.

Rabin, S. (1992). Pooling resources builds private/public partnerships. *Public Relations Journal, 48* (10), 32–34.

Rappaport, J. (1984). Studies in empowerment: Introduction to the issue. In J. Rappaport, C. F. Swift, and R.E. Hess (Eds.), *Studies in empowerment* (pp. 1–7). New York: Haworth Press.

Rappaport, J. (1987). Terms of empowerment/exemplars of prevention: Toward a theory for community psychology. *American Journal of Community Psychology, 15* (2), 121–48.

Rogers, C. (1961). *On becoming a person: A therapist's view of psychotherapy.* Boston: Houghton-Mifflin

Schein, E. H. (1987). *Process consultation: Vol. 2. Lessons for managers and consultants.* Reading, Mass.: Addison-Wesley

Simon, B. (1994). *The empowerment tradition in American social work.* New York: Columbia University Press.

Solomon, B. (1976). *Black empowerment: Social work in oppressed communities.* New York: Columbia University Press.

Solomon, B.B. (1987). Empowerment: Social work in oppressed communities. *Journal of Social Work Practice, 2* (4), 79–91.

Trohanis, P. (2001). *Design considerations for state TA systems.* Chapel Hill: University of North Carolina, FPG Child Development Center, National Early Childhood Technical Assistance System (NECTAS).

Vroon Vandenberg, LLP. (n.d.). *Consultation and Technical Assistance* page. Retrieved February 22, 2005 from http://www.vroonvdb.com/about_consultation.html.

University of North Carolina, School of Public Health. (n.d.). *Institutes and Centers* section, *Technical Assistance and Consultation* page. Retrieved February 22, 2005 from http://www.sph.unc.edu/practice/technical.

Wahl, E., Cahill, M., and Fruchter, N. (1998). *Building capacity: A review of technical assistance strategies*. New York: Institute for Education and Social Policy, New York University.

Weiner, B. (1986). An *attributional theory of motivation and emotion*. New York: Springer-Verlag.

Whitmore, E. (1990). Empowerment in program evaluation: A case example. *Canadian Social Work Review, 7* (2), 215–29.

Zemke, R., and Zemke, S. (1984). Thirty things we know for sure about adult learning. *Innovation Abstracts, 6* (8), 45–52.

Zimmerman, B.J. (2000). Self-efficacy: An essential motive to learn. *Contemporary Educational Psychology, 25* (1), 82–91.

Chapter Three

Cultural Competence

At the Heart of Capacity Building

■ ■ ■

PEG MCCARTT HESS AND ANDREW BILLINGSLEY

Effectively serving and supporting families requires that professionals, organizations, and communities develop the skills to work with those from diverse backgrounds and varied social cultures. In human service fields, these skills are commonly referred to as cultural competence. It is believed and results have shown that by integrating and transforming knowledge about individuals and groups of people into specific standards, policies, practices, and attitudes used in culturally competent settings, the quality of services is increased and outcomes are enhanced (Black and Mendenhall, 1990; Child Welfare League, n.d.; Rynes and Rosen, 1995).

Within any community, families' experiences and traditions differ. And within any community lies the primary source of knowledge about its own varying cultures. Professionals who assist organizations and communities in building their capacity to serve families must help organizations understand the importance of accessing the community's knowledge about its cultures and identify methods for doing so. In addition, consultants must be engaged in the ongoing process of developing their own cultural competence as well as preparing themselves to assist with the needs and issues that will inevitably arise in relation to the cultural competence of others.

Often one encounters assertions that there are no longer significant racial, ethnic, social class, age, or gender differences that affect the problems that families face, their response to the problems, or the assistance they receive. These assertions must be carefully analyzed. At the same time, professionals must avoid overemphasizing differences, which can contribute to stereotyping. Listening, observing (especially participant observation), and study can help avoid the tendencies to ignore important cultural dimensions on the one hand and to stereotype on the other.

For organizations to develop cultural competence, prime requisites include a sensitive and culturally diverse policy board, staff, and volunteers, as well as policies and practices that reflect and are responsive to the diversity of the population served. Organizational cultural competence also incorporates other elements that are explored in this chapter.

Specifically, in this chapter we

- define culture and cultural competence;
- discuss why cultural competence is an essential component of professional service in contemporary society;
- identify, discuss, and illustrate essential attitudes and actions for professionals, organizations, and communities that aspire to become culturally competent; and
- examine ways in which consultants assist communities and organizations in providing culturally competent programs and services to families.

DEFINING CULTURE AND CULTURAL COMPETENCE

Social scientists have come to appreciate the fact that cultural factors and differences often exert a powerful influence on "how individuals think, feel and behave" (Hines, Garcia-Preto, McGoldrick, Almeida, and Weltman, 1992). Culture, therefore, is inherently influential in the definition of problems to be addressed through social programs (Madison, 1992, cited in SenGupta, Hopson, and Thompson-Robinson, 2004, p. 8); can "influence service outcomes" (Malik and Velazquez, 2002, p. 24); and should be taken into account in program evaluation (American Psychological Association, 2003; Joh, Endo, and Yu 2003; SenGupta, Hopson, and Thompson-Robinson, 2004; Symonette, 2004).

The concept of *culture* refers in general to the "ways of life" followed by a particular body of people. This includes their values, norms, belief systems, ways of thinking and acting, language and other characteristics that are passed down from one generation to the next. Thus, the "manifestations of culture, such as food, music, celebrations, holidays, dance and dress and clothing . . . are rooted in inherent beliefs and value orientations that influence customs, norms, practices, and social institutions, including psychological processes, language, caretaking practices, media, education systems, and organizations" (SenGupta, Hopson, and Thompson-Robinson, 2004, p. 6). Culture, therefore, is a social concept that enables individuals to identify themselves as belonging to particular groups in society (Leigh, 1998).

Traditional cultures tend to vary with the historical, geographic or ecological, and sociopolitical origins of a particular group of people. Thus, national origin, language, race, religion, ethnicity, social class, and gender are among the most common bases for the ascription of *cultural groups*. The coming together of two or more cultural groups for sustained interaction is referred to as *cultural diversity*.

Cultural norms, such as the definition of family, may vary not only between and among groups but within a single group as well. Therefore, even within a cultural group there are cultural factors and norms that must be taken into account when developing an accurate understanding of the group. In addition, professionals and others who are involved with communities and organizations that serve families must be aware that cultural definitions change over time.

While there is an enduring quality to cultures, as Benedict (1934) emphasized many years ago, they are also subject to change over time and under varying circumstances. Cultures are particularly sensitive to changes in environment, technology, and economic conditions. For example, recent demographic trends are substantially changing the cultural mix of the population of the United States. It has been estimated that by 2050, racial and ethnic minorities combined will constitute a numerical majority in the population (Hansen, Pepitone-Arreola-Rockwell, and Greene, 2000). Whites will no longer hold that distinction. Undoubtedly, then, the Europeanization of America will give way to a more complex mosaic of peoples. And where white men once constituted the majority of the labor force in the United States, today more than 80 percent of those entering the work force are women and members of minority groups (Shipp and Davison, 2001). This contributes to greater cultural complexity in the work place and increasingly will require enhanced cultural competence on the part of employers, supervisors, and workers, and thus on the part of all community organizations.

After many years of inattention, the concepts of *cultural competence, cultural sensitivity,* and *cultural responsiveness* have recently been described in the human services literature by a broad range of sources. Professional associations of psychology, social work, and counseling have promulgated ethical guidelines that require members to learn about cultural differences and to be sensitive to those differences in their practice. For example, the National Association of Social Workers *Code of Ethics* advises that social workers should "have a knowledge base of services that are sensitive to clients' cultures and to differences among people and cultural groups" (National Association of Social Workers, 1996, p. 9).

In a national initiative to increase cultural competence, the American Psychological Association established work groups on a wide range of cultural statuses, including age, gender, race, ethnicity, national origin, religion, sexual orientation, disability, language, and socioeconomic status (Hansen, Pepitone-Arreola-Rockwell, and Greene, 2000). Twelve competencies were developed (p. 653), as shown in table 3.1.

TABLE 3.1 Minimal Multicultural Competencies for Practice

1.	Awareness of how one's own cultural heritage, gender, class, ethnic-racial identity, sexual orientation, disability, and age cohort help shape personal values, assumptions, and biases related to identified groups.
2.	Knowledge of how psychological theory, methods of inquiry and professional practices are historically and culturally embedded and how they have changed over time as societal values and political priorities shift.
3.	Knowledge of the history and manifestation of oppression, prejudice, and discrimination in the United States and their psychological sequelae.
4.	Knowledge of sociopolitical influences.
5.	Knowledge of culture-specific diagnostic categories.
6.	Knowledge of such issues as normative values about illness, help-seeking behavior, interactional styles, and worldview of the main groups that the clinician is likely to encounter professionally.
7.	Knowledge of culture-specific assessment procedures and tools and their empirical support.

(continued)

TABLE 3.1 Minimal Multicultural Competencies for Practice (*continued*)

8.	Knowledge of family structures, gender roles, values, beliefs, and worldviews and how they differ across identified groups in the United States, along with their impact on personality formation, developmental outcomes, and manifestations of mental and physical illness.
9.	Ability to accurately evaluate emic (culture-specific) and etic (universal) hypotheses related to clients from identified groups and to develop accurate clinical conceptualizations, including awareness of when clinical issues involve cultural dimensions (APA, 1993) and when theoretical orientation needs to be adapted for more effective work with members of identified groups.
10.	Ability to accurately self-assess one's multicultural competence, including knowing when circumstances (e.g., personal biases; stage of ethnic identity; lack of requisite knowledge, skills, or language fluency; sociopolitical influences) are negatively influencing professional activities and adapting accordingly (e.g., obtaining needed information, consultation, or supervision or referring the client to a more qualified provider.
11.	Ability to modify assessment tools and qualify conclusions appropriately (including empirical support, where available) for use with identified groups.
12.	Ability to design and implement nonbiased, effective treatment plans and interventions for clients from identified groups, including the following:
a.	Ability to assess such issues as clients' level of acculturation, acculturative stress, and stage of gay or lesbian identity development.
b.	Ability to ascertain effects of therapist-client language difference (including use of translators, if necessary) on psychological assessment and intervention.
c.	Ability to establish rapport and convey empathy in culturally sensitive ways (e.g., taking into account culture-bound interpretations of verbal and non-verbal cues, personal space, and eye contact)
d.	Ability to initiate and explore issues of difference between the therapist and the client, when appropriate, and to incorporate these considerations into effective treatment planning.

Source: Hansen, Pepitone-Arreola-Rockwell, and Greene, 2000, p. 653.

CULTURAL COMPETENCE:
TRANSLATING KNOWLEDGE INTO ACTION

Authors who write about cultural competence emphasize the importance of *translating knowledge into action*. To illustrate, item 12 in table 3.1 requires the application of knowledge and awareness or the "ability to implement" knowledge in relevant areas in practice. McPhatter (1997) has defined cultural competence as "the ability to transform knowledge and cultural awareness into health and/or psychosocial interventions that support and sustain healthy client-system functioning within the appropriate cultural context" (p. 261). Similarly, drawing upon her own earlier work and that of Hodges (1991), Pinderhughes (1995) defines cultural competence as including the following abilities that reflect particular perspectives and capacities:

- the ability to respect and appreciate the values, beliefs, and practices of all clients, including those who are culturally different [from the practitioner], and to perceive such individuals through their own cultural lens rather than that of the practitioner;
- knowledge of the specific values, beliefs, and cultural practices of clients;
- the ability to be comfortable with differences in others and to avoid becoming trapped in anxious or defensive behavior in response to differences;
- the ability to change false beliefs, assumptions, and stereotypes;
- the ability to think flexibly and to recognize that one's own way of thinking and behavior is not the only way to think and behave; and
- the ability to behave flexibly, as demonstrated by the readiness to take the steps required to sort through general knowledge about cultural groups and to perceive the specific ways in which such knowledge applies or does not apply to a given client.

(p. 133)

The authors also have found the Child Welfare League of America's definition of cultural competence a useful one: "the ability of individuals and systems to respond respectfully and effectively to people of all cultures, classes, races, ethnic backgrounds, sexual orientations, and faiths or religions in a manner that recognizes, affirms, and values the worth of individuals, families, tribes, and communities and protects and preserves the dignity of each" (Child Welfare League of America, n.d.). This definition emphasizes *response* and is sufficiently broad and flexible to encourage the recognition of gender, social class, and age as cultural variables as well. These characteristics are cultural in the sense that they may well expose persons sharing them to common experiences and the development of similar attitudes or beliefs.

While sexual orientation is among the most recently recognized dimension of cultural diversity, the value of perceiving it as a cultural dimension is recognized in practice and in the literature. A group of physicians and psychologists in Boston found that the recognition of sexual orientation as a cultural phenomenon has had positive results in treatment. They found that "increased expertise and cultural competence in lesbian, gay, bisexual and transsexual care led to the expansion of medical services to address broader community concerns" (Mayer, Appelbaum, and Rogers, 2001, p. 6).

Cultural competence, then, is knowledge and awareness in action. It involves the capacity or ability of individuals and professionals to function flexibly and effectively in carrying forth a mission with knowledge, recognition, and awareness of their own culture as well as the culture of another, in a manner by which the two may interact and be cognizant of the consequences of such interactions. As many have emphasized, the achievement of cultural competence is not an outcome but rather an ongoing process (Isaacs and Benjamin 1998; Malik and Velazquez, 2002; Nash, 1993).

With regard to cultural competence, we are reminded by Pinderhughes and others that practitioners who would become culturally competent must be prepared for information and experiences that go against the expectations of professional experience or conventional wisdom. For example, one careful study (Julian, McKenry, and McKelvey, 1994) of cultural variations in parenting among four major cultural groups—Caucasians, African Americans, Hispanic Americans, and Asian Americans—examined married-couple families. Using data from the National Survey of Families and Households, the authors reported the following findings: When social class was controlled, there were no significant differences among the various groups regarding parenting attitudes, parental behaviors, and parental involvement with children. They also found, however, that parents in all three minority groups expressed greater emphasis on their children exercising "self control" and "succeeding in school" than the Caucasian parents. These findings are useful for cultural diversity and cultural competence training because the authors developed a complex design and avoided the more common practice of comparing middle-class whites with working-class blacks.

CULTURALLY COMPETENT ORGANIZATIONS

Others have applied the knowledge, attitudinal/value, and behavioral components of cultural competence to organizations. For example, the Child Welfare League of America stresses that all those who work in the field of child welfare must "become culturally competent in the unique family customs, perspectives, and cultural histories of the specific groups we serve. We must also build appropriate checkpoints into our policies and practices to ensure that we identify culturally relevant issues, and implement services in a manner appropriate to them. Thus, we must accept culture and ethnicity as a central focus in policy making and in planning and providing services to children and their families" (1993). To support this focus, CWLA published the *Cultural Competence Self-Assessment Instrument* (1993), designed to help agencies measure cultural competence in policy-making, administrative procedures, and practices and to guide agencies in their review and assessment of operational and programmatic functions. Items are also included for clients to assess the cultural competence of the services they receive.

BUILDING THE CAPACITY FOR CULTURAL COMPETENCE

Organizations and communities that are interested in meaningful program outcomes for the families they serve must attend to the cultural contexts of the lives of program participants and of providers. Becoming culturally competent requires commitment and action at all levels of an organization. Therefore, coaches[1] supporting organizational efforts in capacity building must keep cultural issues on the agenda. Without focused attention, program leadership and staff are likely to give only initial or periodic attention to issues of diversity as particular issues arise (e.g., is the service location accessible to diverse groups of participants?). Evaluations have found that when cultural competence is reflected in program design and staff practices, service effectiveness and participant satisfaction are enhanced (Black and Mendenhall, 1990; Rynes and Rosen, 1995). Therefore, coaches must support and monitor the inclusion of such concerns in capacity-building efforts. The institutionalization of cultural knowledge

---

1. Throughout this volume, the term "coach" is used interchangeably with the term "capacity-building consultants" who provide technical assistance to community groups or organizations to support and strengthen families.

can then occur as the organization's leadership encourages or mandates that cultural knowledge be incorporated into program planning, implementation, and evaluation.

A number of elements are essential for organizations that aspire to become culturally competent. These elements are supported in the literature (Cross, Bazron, Dennis, and Isaacs, 1989; Isaacs and Benjamin, 1998) as well as by our own practice. These include

- developing cultural knowledge and awareness of the experiences of self and others;
- recognizing, identifying, and valuing diversity within the community;
- giving ongoing attention to the organization's cultural self-assessment and to self-awareness of administrators, staff, board members, and other constituencies;
- understanding the dynamics of differences when cultures intersect;
- changing policies, practices, and organizational resources that reflect false beliefs, assumptions, and stereotypes; and
- flexibly adapting to diversity.

Developing Cultural Knowledge and Awareness of the Experiences of Self and Others

As coaches who assist organizations and communities in building their capacity to better serve families, giving purposive attention to cultural competence *in our own practice* must precede and parallel our interactions with organizational leaders, staff, and program participants. Otherwise, our focus on cultural competence will be shallow and ineffective. For example, we must develop self-awareness regarding our own ethnic and cultural identities and statuses, including both privilege and oppression (Franks, 1999). We must develop an understanding of our own cultural values and norms, particularly those regarding power and authority, self-disclosure, conflict, decision making, success and failure, appropriate behavior in the workplace, group/individualism, time, and space. We must be willing to examine the question, "Who do those that we are seeking to communicate with and engage perceive [us] as being?" and recognize that until otherwise demonstrated, we are who we are perceived to be by those with whom we consult (Symonette, 2004, p. 100). Our cultural competence enables us to understand the importance of this question and to address it authentically. Thus, culturally competent consultants must anticipate, carefully examine, and be prepared to appropriately address the similarities and differences between their own values and norms and those of both the colleagues with whom they consult and the families served within their communities.

Patton (1985) emphasizes that the limitations of our own perspectives, behaviors, and values are often obscured due to the power of our own cultural lens. Because of this, the examination of one's own and others' cultural values and norms often can occur most effectively in a diverse group where a commitment to ongoing development of cultural competence is shared and where open discussion and questioning can occur.

One of the factors that must be understood in efforts to build cultural competence among institutions and professionals is that the white Americans who have dominated much of life in the United States during the nineteenth and twentieth centuries are not removed from the requirement for cultural self-awareness. White Americans who come in contact with the cultures of "minority groups" often ignore the fact that they, too, have cultures that need to be understood and managed in helping relations with persons from their own and from other cultural groupings. Hess and Hess have pointed out that being of European descent does not in itself provide a homogenous culture (2001). One publication (Giordano and McGoldrick, 1996) reported that there are "53 categories of European-Americans," a term used interchangeably with "White ethnics" (p. 427). Even so, there are some common values that have been historically associated with European descent. Among these are self-sufficiency, strength, self-discipline, and self-control; an orientation toward work, privacy, and the future; child-centeredness; and the like (Hess and Hess, 2001). Professionals must examine these values, the extent to which they exist in other cultures, and the ways in which rigid adherence to these values and efforts to insure that others also adopt them may be obstacles to effective collaboration with, providing services to, and receiving services from persons of other cultures (Hess and Hess, 2001).

Professionals who would strive for cultural competence in their practice must reach beyond suppositions that may grow out of the unexamined aspects of their own culture, the cultures in which they have received primary and secondary (professional) socialization, and the culture of their employing agency. One faulty practice, still much too common in social science research, is to compare samples of privileged whites with samples of nonprivileged minorities and to draw conclusions about the difference in values in these two distinct populations, generally with the white sample reflecting "more appropriate values" and the minority sample less so. Despite the fact that the concept of *social class* has generally shown its utility in distinguishing populations, this knowledge is often set aside when it comes to comparing whites and minorities on almost any dimension of accepted or functional attitudes and behaviors.

KNOWLEDGE ABOUT AND AWARENESS OF SELF. Preparation for multi- or cross-cultural practice has often focused on learning about those *different from self*. Increasingly, however, learning about *self* has been recognized as a critical first step to developing cultural competence (Wheeler, Walters, Hess, Franks, and Sheiman, 1999). Franks (1999) emphasizes that "self-awareness implies more than just an awareness of one's values, attitudes, and world view. It implies understanding self in relation to within- and between-group differences, identity development, power and privilege statuses, and the experience of multiple statuses" (p. 1). Thus, as noted earlier, consultants must engage in activities that expand their own self-awareness and cultural competence as well as develop sensitive and effective ways to assist leaders and service providers in the organizations with which they consult. Consistent with this, SenGupta, Hopson, and Thompson-Robinson (2004) stress, "accomplishing cultural competence in one's practice does not mean abandoning one's cultural background, worldview, training, and skill sets. Accomplishing cultural competence requires increased and critical self-reflection as the first building block" (p. 14). Many resources are available to facilitate such efforts (Kumpfer, 2000; Leigh, 1998; Nash, 2003; Webb, 2001b).

For consultants, a core area for self-awareness is that of one's own assumptions and expectations about problem definition and resolution and decisions regarding seeking and receiving help. Webb (2001a), in writing about the strains and challenges of culturally diverse practice, emphasizes cultural differences in worldviews and help-seeking patterns. She explores the different expectations regarding the need for help and the type of help desired between proponents of the linear worldview, which depends on cause-and-effect thinking regarding problems and their solutions, and those who hold a relational worldview, which emphasizes restoration of "balance and harmony among the various cognitive, emotional, physical, and spiritual components of the person's life" (p. 347). Awareness of one's own culturally derived assumptions and expectations and of the ways in which they may be similar or different from those with whom one consults (i.e., consultation, technical assistance or service) is necessary in order to acknowledge, understand, and appropriately respond to cultural differences.

KNOWLEDGE ABOUT AND EXPERIENCES WITH OTHERS. We have found it useful to conceptualize cultural knowledge on a continuum of proximity to and experience with the culture. At one end of the continuum is knowledge that is derived from studying published knowledge about various cultures and cultural knowledge derived from training and education. While such knowledge is valuable, it may lack the component of personal interaction and experience that enriches and structures one's understanding. Midway along the continuum is knowledge derived from conversations with others about their experiences. At the other end of the continuum is knowledge derived from direct and sustained day-to-day experiences (i.e., living and working in other cultures). Some professionals develop the knowledge essential to cultural competence by reading about various cultures, enrolling in courses, and attending workshops and seminars. Others, as recommended by Leigh (1998), develop cultural knowledge through friendly conversations as well as by systematically inquiring about others' cultural experiences.

Still, others derive knowledge that supports their cultural competence through active participation in cultural activities and through living and working for extended periods in cultures other than their own. To illustrate, the director of a multiservice center located in a community with a growing number of recent immigrants from Central and South America chose to spend several weeks studying Spanish in one of the countries from which many of the immigrants in his community had come. By living with several families and immersing himself in the culture, he returned to his community work not only with an enhanced ability to communicate with program participants but with greater cultural awareness and competence. Knowledge derived through personally experiencing another culture is particularly useful in developing the ability to change false beliefs, assumptions, and stereotypes. Having knowledge derived from multiple sources, (e.g., study, interactions with others, and immersion in cultures different than one's own), most fully enhances the depth and breadth of one's comprehension and ability to adapt one's behavior.

KNOWLEDGE DEVELOPMENT AND FORMAL TRAINING FOR CULTURAL COMPETENCE. The development of cultural knowledge within organizations that serve families must be an ongoing and consistently high priority. As Shipp and Davison (2001) have pointed out, enhancing positive responses to diversity requires more than the individual practitioner, it requires the entire agency or helping system.

Capacity-building consultants can support such culturally competent efforts by identifying and providing resources (e.g., materials that identify and discuss diverse family needs and experiences); assisting organizations in identifying appropriate training opportunities for staff, board members, and others; and helping organizations draw upon the expertise, knowledge, and experiences of program participants as well as of local community members and key informants.

Many approaches to training in cultural competence have been developed. The challenges of such training include identifying relevant curriculum and training content, minimizing defensive attitudes and behaviors on the part of training participants, making ongoing learning and application of training a goal, and assuring that organizations protect participants' time for training. The wide use of training for cultural competence in human services agencies has been documented. For example, Isaacs and Benjamin surveyed the states' child mental health systems over a five-year period beginning in 1991 and subsequently described the states' approaches to ongoing intensive training in cultural competence (1998).

Although formal study and evaluation of the impact of training upon services provided has been limited, formal training for cultural competence has been found to be effective. For example, the New York State Office of Mental Health developed an intensive three-day training module for direct care staff. During the course of a recent year, almost 4,000 staff members were provided this voluntary training. Pre- and post-test training evaluations based upon self-report were given to measure cultural competence. The post-test showed statistically significant results in the areas of increases in communication and interaction, respect for receivers of care, and an increase in cultural competence levels (Way, Stone, Schwager, Wagoner, and Bassman, 2002).

Recognizing, Identifying, and Valuing Diversity Within the Community

Profound changes continue to occur in the demographics of families in the United States as well as in racial, ethnic, and religious differences in marriage and family practices. To illustrate, in the United States in 1998, the proportion of families in which both spouses work became the majority (51 percent) of all married couple families, compared with 33 percent in 1976 (U.S. Census Bureau, 2000). Although the number of single mothers has recently remained fairly constant, the number of single fathers grew 25 percent between 1995 and 1998 (U.S. Census Bureau, 1998); and by 2003, 9.8 million school-aged children (5–17) spoke a language other than English at home (U.S. Census Bureau, 2003). As these and other trends have occurred, traditional human service programs have necessarily reexamined the types of services needed by diverse families as well as the appropriate design and delivery of services to support them.

In working toward enhanced organizational cultural competence, consultants help organizations explore the degree to which the diversity in the communities they serve is identified, understood, and valued by consistently posing questions such as the following:

- Is the community's population changing and, if so, in what ways?
- What strengths and resources are present in various cultures within the community?
- What service needs are present?
- What disparities can be identified in current service access, timeliness, and effectiveness?
- What cultural norms and traditions should be taken into account in ongoing service design, delivery, and evaluation?

Each community organization must continuously assess its mission, policies, programs, services, and resources in light of the continuously changing nature of its cultural context. However, in doing so, those engaged in assessment must be vigilant for the influence and limitations of their own cultural lens or perspectives as they answer questions such as those posed above, i.e., "What strengths and resources are present in various cultures within the community?"

SenGupta, Hopson, and Thompson-Robinson (2004) stress that one way in which cultural values are expressed "is in how social problems and the programs intended to address them are conceptualized. It is also in this context that one needs to be especially aware of the dangers of imposition, misinterpretation, and misrepresentations of values, of viewing a particular context with a different cultural lens in program design" (p. 8). These authors emphasize that the dominant culture's interpretation of reality has historically perpetuated the myth of deficits, framing programs for groups termed as underprivileged, chronically unemployed, at-risk, and chronically homeless. This negative outcome in program planning and design is best prevented through the full and timely inclusion of community members and potential program consumers in defining the community problems and needs that organizational programs intend to address.

Ongoing Attention to the Organization's Cultural Self-Assessment and Self-Awareness

Professionals who would help an organization to build capacities of families and communities need to be aware of the organization's culture and sensitive to it. Cultural self-assessment incorporates an examination of the individual and collective knowledge about diverse cultures within the organization, the individual and collective assumptions and beliefs held about diverse cultural practices and norms, and the ability of the organization's staff and leadership to translate knowledge about the cultures of program participants into culturally appropriate policies, programs, and practices. Resources are available to assist in completing a systematic cultural self-assessment. These include CWLA's *Cultural Competence Self-Assessment Instrument* (1993) and Mason's *Cultural Competence Self-Assessment Questionnaire* (1995) for organizations and, for individuals, Chadiha, Miller-Cribbs, and Wilson-Klar's *Similarities and Differences Questionnaire* (1997) and Paniagua's *Self-Evaluation of Biases and Prejudices Scale* (1998). A one-time assessment will not be sufficient; annual or periodic cultural competence updates are necessary. A thorough assessment taps the perspectives and experiences of agency-affiliated persons in multiple roles.

For example, CWLA recommends that the *Cultural Competence Self-Assessment Instrument* should be completed by all agency personnel, including those in administrative, managerial, program/policy development, service delivery, and informational and referral roles and all board or advisory committee members. In addition, CWLA recommends that a random selection of former clients be surveyed. The assessment process must include steps for thoughtful interpretation of the data generated as well as for the development of an agency plan to address the weaknesses and other issues identified related to cultural diversity and cultural competence.

As culturally competent consultants engage with organizations in examining data regarding program participants' experiences, they often have the opportunity to assist organizations in identifying and decreasing disparities in service access and outcome and in addressing issues of social and economic justice. In addition, issues may be identified with regard to the agency's mission and goals, selection and orientation of board members, relationship with the community, or staff recruitment, training, retention, and supervision. As Nash (1993) emphasizes, organizations that "want to attract and retain the best talent in the field must demonstrate the ability to provide a safe and comfortable environment, where difference is valued" (p. 42). Priorities must be set and strategies developed to accomplish needed changes.

UNDERSTANDING THE DYNAMICS OF DIFFERENCE

When cultures clash, misunderstandings and impasses are likely to occur. In consultants' own work with organizations, it is important to anticipate the ways in which their personal cultural norms may clash with those of the organization and its members and reflect upon questions such as:

- Are there similarities and/or differences between one's own personal cultural norms and those of the organization and its members in the ways in which power and authority are viewed? In the degree to which self-disclosure is valued? In preferred approaches to conflict and to conflict resolution? In preferred approaches to decision making? In definitions of success and failure?
- How do the cultural norms of the consultant's own organization differ from those of the organizations with which they consult?

For example, in many instances, consultants are based in academic institutions, with priorities and values that differ from those of a community-based service organization. Consultants may also have extensive experience in program evaluation with priorities and values that differ from those of the practitioner staff of service organizations with which they consult. Culturally competent consultants will anticipate and seek to decrease the potential negative effects of such differences.

In a parallel process, consultants should assist organizations in identifying and addressing the ways in which the cultural norms and expectations of the organization's leadership and staff may clash both *within* the organization and *between* the organizational leadership/staff and the program participants and diverse families in the community. For example, a comprehensive community initiative to promote school readiness through multiple programs aimed at early childhood development sought to reach recent Latino immigrant families. Several families were hesitant to send their children to the early education programs because they doubted the quality of the programs. One symbol of quality in their Central American home communities is that the children would wear uniforms when attending the program. Absence of uniforms meant the program was basically a child-care center, not a program focused on education or development. The program staff had a cross-cultural dilemma: although the Latino immigrant families would prefer uniforms for preschool children, many of the other families, long-term residents in the U.S., would resist uniforms. The program staff opted not to require uniforms for children attending the program but did recognize the need for revising their outreach to Latino immigrant families with preschool-aged children to further clarify the program's educational goals and value. Consultants must assist organizations in answering the following question: How can such cross-cultural conflict be anticipated, addressed, and resolved in ways that increase accessibility of all community residents to services, promote program growth, and encourage collective growth toward cultural competence?

Changing Policies, Practices, and Resources
That Reflect False Beliefs and Assumptions

Pinderhughes (1995) emphasizes that a culturally competent professional is able to recognize that one's own way of thinking and behaving is not the only way to think and behave and able to change one's own false beliefs, assumptions, and stereotypes. For both individuals and organizations, this can be a particularly difficult aspect of achieving cultural competence. Unfortunately organizations can enhance the ability to value diversity, assess the cultural competence of their policies and practices, and further develop individual and collective cultural knowledge *without* making a serious commitment to change policies and practices based upon their increased knowledge and awareness. As Symonette (2004) emphasizes, "Structural diversity and access issues are critical, but they simply lay the foundation—necessary but not sufficient. Multicultural development requires movement beyond tolerance, accommodation, and pressure to fit in toward a focus on changes in policies, processes, and practices in order to genuinely invite and engage the full spectrum of diverse voices, perspectives, experiences and peoples" (p. 96)

Large, more traditional organizations in particular, such as governmental agencies, find it difficult to confront the challenges inherent in change, in doing things differently than they have always been done, and in authentically implementing change. In assessing the foundation built for cultural competence in the United States, Isaacs and Benjamin (1998) stress that "a political party change, a change in commissioner, the ending of a grant, or even the vacating of a specialized multicultural job position can undo all the work that has been started in a state. One of the major elements of cultural competence is that it becomes institutionalized . . . integrated within the mission and ongoing operation of the organization" (p. 86). They identify thirteen core components that need to be in place to build a solid infrastructure for cultural competence development in an agency or organization. These include the development of mission statements, definitions, policies, and procedures that explicitly state the agency's cultural competence values and principles; the inclusion of cultural competence requirements and measures in the development of certification, licensure, and contract standards; evaluation and research activities that provide feedback about progress and guide future steps; and the commitment of both human and financial agency resources.

Vignette: Infusing Cultural Competence—An Important Lesson Learned in Strategic Grant Making

A large community foundation embarked in a new direction with regard to grant making. The new approach included targeting key community issues through defined strategic initiatives, making larger grants to address the strategic issues, and emphasizing the importance of outcomes through a capacity-building process. The four strategic initiatives selected by the foundation emerged from an intensive community planning effort. The selected initiatives addressed (1) strengthening families with preschool children, (2) promoting harmony among diverse populations, (3) enabling people with economic and other challenges to improve their situations, and (4) promoting healthy youth development.

As part of the resources to each initiative, the foundation provided evaluation support through a team of evaluators. The evaluation process engaged the grantees in a participatory evaluation process focused on building organizational capacity to monitor performance, continuously improve quality, and report outcomes. As part of the evaluative process, the grantees met regularly in interagency and interorganizational groups within each of the four initiative areas to reflect on lessons learned.

Across all four initiatives, commendable levels of positive outcomes were obtained, yet each initiative struggled. For example, preschool children had noted improvements in developmental progress; however, the initiative was challenged when an increasing number of children from Hispanic/Latino and other diverse backgrounds became recipients of the program services. Like the preschool program, the youth development initiative demonstrated progress in improving youth development and parental support. However, both programs had difficulty reaching the youth that really needed the services offered. Cultural issues (program content and process) as well as practical issues (e.g., transportation) were challenges. The initiative addressing the needs of adults with chronic economic issues found itself working with people suffering from addictions, domestic violence, poverty, and mental and physical disabilities. Extensive support was needed to address the personal needs of the program recipients. Dropout rates were extremely high. The initiative ultimately served a very small number of participants extremely well but clearly did not reach

(*continued*)

the expected outcomes of the funder. The initiative focused on bridging relationships among diverse groups also had challenges. While successful at bringing diverse groups together, the outcomes of the initiative were fairly "intangible" and extremely difficulty to document.

Across all four initiatives, the foundation learned many lessons about strategic grant making. They also learned an important lesson about cultural competence. Cultural competence cannot be set aside as a separate initiative (e.g., building harmony among diverse groups). In this strategic grant-making effort, all four initiatives brought together diverse groups and were challenged with helping the initiative to meet its goals and objectives. For example, a white, middle-class approach to preschool education needed to be adjusted to facilitate the involvement of newly immigrated Hispanic/Latino families. Supporting long-term, chronically unemployed black males required attention to issues of personal and institutional racism. Youth development required attention to cultural preferences among the diverse members of the community. In the one initiative set aside to bring diverse groups together, a large challenge was defining strategically a meaningful way to bridge the involvement of diverse groups. The funder learned that all four initiatives directly or contextually addressed issues of cultural competence. From the "culturally bound" definition of family, to strategies for encouraging economic independence, to skill building with youth, the identification of cultural issues and the development of culturally responsive programming are keys to program success. As a group of initiatives, all four shared a service delivery focus. The need to become culturally competent directly affects service delivery.

Although implicit in the broad focus of the foundation's grant-making approach, there was no stated priority on developing culturally competent programming. The foundation realized that the absence of cultural competence approaches would affect the overall value of their grant making. To have a directed focus on cultural competence would help ensure a priority on issues of diversity across all program efforts. Funding a single initiative focused directly on cultural competency could not meet the broad needs of the larger initiative.

Building on research that encourages collaborative partnerships as avenues to address mutual goals, the foundation realized the importance of using their grant-making efforts to strategically bring together diverse

(*continued*)

groups to tackle community issues. By doing so, they would be working to build intergroup relations among diverse groups as well as enhance the likelihood of establishing culturally responsive programming. The foundation realized the importance of infusing cultural competency and building intergroup relationships throughout all funded programs.

Consequently, the foundation revised its requirements for strategic grants. Grantees were required to address how diverse groups would be included in all aspects of the funded project (e.g., board membership, project leadership, project participants, program strategies). These requirements were not only for programs addressing specific race/ethnic and diversity issues but for all funded efforts. The foundation realized that expertise and knowledge of diverse cultures is needed to strategically affect community change. The foundation also looked for ways to build cultural competence within its own organization (e.g., policies, practices) and to facilitate it within the local nonprofit community.

DEVELOPING AGENCY RESOURCES AND MATERIALS. As organizations attempt to make their practice more culturally competent, staff members often identify the need to develop new, more culturally sensitive and effective materials (Nash, 1993). Coaches may facilitate this process and identify possible resources. Hess and Jackson (1995) have recommended that agencies apply the technological concept "user-friendly" in developing "family-friendly" environments that ease families' interactions with organizations and staff members. They note that an agency communicates its commitment to serve diverse races, ethnic groups, and family forms through agency brochures and advertisements, responsiveness to telephone inquiries, the nature of initial face-to-face transactions between families and agency staff, and freedom from stereotypical and discriminatory wording and categories in written and verbal communication.

For example, it is important to be mindful that the simple questions concerning family membership can be posed in ways that shame or alienate family members or encourage deception (Hess and Jackson, 1995). Questions asked of families verbally or on an organization's forms may either convey culturally limited assumptions about how families are constituted or instead encourage clients to openly acknowledge their family's unique membership and set of relationships and roles. For example, questions should anticipate that children may be biological, step-, adopted, foster, extended family/kin, or godchildren, and that children's caregiver may be a single mother, father, grandmother, aunt, godparent, or family friend, or there may be two or more caregivers, such as mother and father, mother and mother, mother and aunt, or grandmother, grandfather, and aunt.

Resources are available to guide consultants and community organizations in their efforts to develop culturally appropriate messages and materials. For example, a Technical Assistance Bulletin from the National Clearinghouse for Alcohol and Drug Information (Wright, 1994) emphasizes that "cultural sensitivity should be a factor in the design of all organizational communications, including speeches and news releases, not just in targeted public service announcements, brochures, and special media campaigns." This resource identifies common mistakes in creating culturally sensitive and effective materials, e.g., failing to involve members of the target group in the development and selection of materials, ignoring variations within a racial or ethnic group, and using terms or language that offends the target group. Relying solely on print is another mistake. Potential program participants may prefer oral communications and therefore could best be reached through radio and television programs (Malik and Velazquez, 2002) or through audiotapes (Nash, 1993).

Another area in which resources often are lacking is that of appropriate evaluation instruments. For example, consultants and program staff consistently encounter challenges as they seek outcome measures that are culturally relevant. Many standardized instruments have not been normed or tested with diverse populations or do not include relevant items. To illustrate, most work- and career-related tools were developed for high school and college graduates; as a consequence, reliable and valid measures to assess work motivation among chronically unemployed youth and adults from low-income populations can be difficult to find. But program staff members and funding organizations, such as community foundations, are often interested to know whether their programs have affected work motivation as well as actual employment status.

Cultural competence in evaluation, however, goes beyond the appropriateness of evaluation instruments. SenGupta, Hopson, and Thompson-Robinson (2004) emphasize that "one hallmark of evaluative responsiveness . . . is the evaluator's active recognition, appreciation, and incorporation of culturally related contextual factors into his or her practice. The contextual factors include many of the more readily discussed dimensions of culture, including the demographics and some aspects of socioeconomic factors. But these factors also include the less spoken issues of power, institutional racism, and social justice" (p. 11). Inclusion of such factors calls for the use of multiple evaluation methods, particularly of qualitative methods, as discussed in chapter 6, which focuses on self-evaluation for organizations.

LOCATION OF SERVICES. Organizations also demonstrate respect for diverse families through their selection, arrangement, and design of physical space (Germain, 1981). Ongoing cultural assessment should address the accessibility of programs and services to community residents and explore the need to locate or relocate services in settings that community families are comfortable entering, such as churches (Solomon, 1985), schools, or clients' homes, where clients may feel more empowered to play an active role (Gutheil, 1992).

Flexibly Adapting to Diversity

As emphasized throughout this chapter, consultants must encourage organizations to develop mechanisms through which *continuous* self-assessment of the organization's cultural competence occurs and through which the relevance of programs to diverse families in the community is continually examined, evaluated, and addressed. It must be understood that as communities and organizations change, the specific knowledge, attitudes, and skills required for cultural competence will continue to change, and program policies and practice may also require change. The inclusion of diverse program staff, program advisors, program participants, and community residents in ongoing, recurrent program monitoring, evaluation, and planning activities will greatly enhance the likelihood that attention will be given to the need to adapt to diversity. Conner (2004) emphasizes that doing so also increases "multicultural validity" in program evaluation.

Consultants must also anticipate that their own cultural competence may vary as they work with different organizations and communities over time. Thus, again paralleling the experience of organizations, consultants will need to continue their own self-assessment and knowledge development and may in some situations need to include other consultants in a team approach to assure cultural competence and sensitivity.

OBSTACLES TO DEVELOPING CULTURAL COMPETENCE

There are numerous obstacles to developing cultural competence, many of which have been described above. The contributors to this volume have identified three interrelated obstacles that frequently have interfered with the development of cultural competence in the organizations with which they have consulted: time, organizational leadership, and commitment of various stakeholders. Although the first, lack of time, often reflects insufficient resources, it may also reflect a lack of commitment to cultural competence by organizational, community, or funding stakeholders. When there is a lack of commitment, time is not allocated for the tasks described in this chapter, including time for self- and organizational cultural assessment, time for the development of culturally relevant knowledge, and time for exploring the cultural experiences of those employed by and served by the organization. Private and public funding bodies often give lip service to the importance of culturally competent programs and services but will not provide funding for consultation, training, and other ongoing activities that contribute to the development of an organization's cultural competence.

Leadership, or the lack thereof, is another frequently encountered obstacle, as Shipp and Davison (2001, p. 1) note. In many areas, the challenge is no longer the creation of diverse organizations; these are evolving naturally because of changing demographics. Too often, however, leaders view diversity as a thorn in the side, as a potential source of distress for the organization rather than a source of strength. Their efforts to deal with diversity are reactive instead of proactive. Organizational leaders may merely try to toe the line of political correctness. Shipp and Davison identify stages of diversity development through which leaders themselves may move. In the first stage, leaders are practically oblivious to diversity issues; in the fifth, leaders are able to "recognize and use the full potential of all the diverse individuals in their organizations. Leaders who do this effectively are *functionally diverse*" (p. 3).

When organizational and community leaders are themselves open to developing cultural competence, the commitment of time and other organizational resources is less likely to be an obstacle. As long as a community organization's leadership, including members of the policy board, is "practically oblivious to diversity issues" (Shipp and Davison, 2001, p. 3), the organization remains vulnerable to cultural incompetence despite good-faith efforts to increase the cultural competence of program and service staff. Therefore, as a critical component of the development of an organization's cultural competence, consultants must skillfully engage organizational and community leaders in the process.

CONCLUSIONS

Professionals who assist organizations and communities in building their capacity to serve families better must continually develop their own cultural competence and be alert and sensitive to the need for the further development of cultural competence by those with whom they consult. As communities and organizations change, the knowledge, attitudes, and skills required for cultural competence will continue to change, and program policies and practices may also require change. As many have emphasized (Isaacs and Benjamin, 1998; Malik and Valazquez, 2002; Nash, 1993), the development of cultural competence is not an end to be achieved by professionals and by community organizations, but rather an ongoing process. The obstacles of time, organizational leadership, and commitment of various stakeholders must be repeatedly addressed over time in order to assure that the process is not neglected.

References

American Psychological Association. (2003). Guidelines on multicultural education, training, research, practice, and organizational change for psychologists. *American Psychologist, 58* (5), 377–402.

Benedict, R. (1934). *Patterns of culture*. New York: Houghton Mifflin.

Black, J., and Mendenhall, M. (1990). Cross-cultural training effectiveness: A review and a theoretical framework for future research, *Academy of Management Review, 15* (1), 113–36.

Chadiha, L., Miller-Cribbs, J., and Wilson-Klar, D. (1997). *Human diversity content in social work education: A collection of course outlines with content on racial, ethnic, and cultural diversity.* Alexandria, Va.: Council on Social Work Education.

Child Welfare League of America. (1993). *Cultural competence self-assessment instrument.* Washington, D.C.: Child Welfare League of America. (Revised 2002 edition available.)

Child Welfare League of America. (n.d.). *Cultural Competence Defined.* Retrieved March 29, 2004, from http://www.cwla.org/programs/culturalcompetence/culturalabout.html.

Conner, R. (2004). Developing and implementing cultural competent evaluation: A discussion of multicultural validity in two HIV prevention programs for Latinos. In M. Thompson-Robinson, R. Hopson, and S. SenGupta (eds.). *In search of cultural competence in evaluation: Toward principles and practices* (pp. 51–65), San Francisco: Jossey-Bass.

Cross, T., Bazron, B., Dennis, K., and Isaacs, M. (1989). *Towards a culturally competent system of care: A monograph on effective services for minority children who are severely emotionally disturbed.* Washington, D.C.: CASSP Technical Assistance Center, Georgetown University Child Development Center.

Franks, C. (1999). *Helms' theory of white racial identity development and the relevance for the social work profession.* Unpublished paper.

Germain, C. (1981). The physical environment and social work practice. In A. Maluccio (Ed.), *Promoting competence in clients* (pp. 103–24). New York: The Free Press.

Giordano, J., and McGoldrick, M. (1996). European families: An overview. In M. McGoldrick, J. Giordano, and J. Pearce (Eds.), *Ethnicity and family therapy* (2nd ed., pp. 427–41). New York: Guilford Press.

Gutheil, I. (1992). Considering the physical environment: An essential component of good practice. *Social Work, 37,* 391–96.

Hansen, N. D., Pepitone-Arreola-Rockwell, F., and Greene, A. F. (2000). Multicultural competence: Criteria and case examples. *Professional Psychology: Research and Practice, 31*(6), 652–660.

Hess, P., and Hess, H. (2001). Parenting in European American/white families. In N. Webb (Ed.), *Culturally diverse parent-child and family relationships: A guide for social workers and other practitioners* (pp. 307–33). New York: Columbia University Press.

Hess, P., and Jackson, H. (1995). Practice with and on behalf of families. In C. Meyer and M. Mattaini (Eds.), *The foundations of social work practice* (pp. 126–55). Washington, D.C.: NASW Press.

Hines, P., Garcia-Preto, N., McGoldrick, M., Almeida, R., and Weltman, S. (1992). Intergenerational relationships across cultures. *Journal of Contemporary Human Services, 6,* 323–38.

Hodges, V. (1991). Providing culturally sensitive intensive family preservation services to ethnic minority families. In E. Tracy, D. Haapala, J. Kinney, and P. Pecora (Eds.), *Intensive family preservation services: An instructional sourcebook* (pp. 95–116). Cleveland, Ohio: Mandel School of Applied Social Sciences, Case Western Reserve University.

Isaacs, M., and Benjamin, M. (1998). *Towards a culturally competence system of care: Vol. 3. The state of the states: Responses to cultural competence and diversity in child mental health.* Washington, D.C.: National Technical Assistance Center for Children's Mental Health.

Joh, T., Endo, T., and Yu, H. D. (2003). *Voices from the field: Health and evaluation leaders on multicultural evaluation.* Woodland Hills, Calif.: California Endowment Foundation.

Julian, T., McKenry, P., and McKelvey, M. W. (1994). Cultural variations in parenting: Perceptions of Caucasian, African-American, Hispanic, and Asian-American parents. *Family Relations, 43,* 30–37.

Kumpfer, K. L. (2000). Strengthening family involvement in school substance abuse programs. In W. B. Hansen, S. M. Giles, and M. D. Fearnow-Kenney (Eds.). *Improving prevention effectiveness* (chapter 11, pp. 127-40). Greensboro, N.C.: Tanglewood Research.

Leigh, J. (1998). *Communicating for cultural competence.* Boston: Allyn and Bacon.

Madison, A. M. (Ed.). (1992). *Minority Issues in Evaluation.* New Directions for Program Evaluation, 53. San Francisco: Jossey-Bass.

Malik, S., and Velazquez, J. (2002). Cultural competence and the new Americans. *Children's Voice, 11* (4), 24–26.

Mason, J. (1995). *Cultural competence self assessment questionnaire: A manual for users.* Portland, Ore.: Research and Training Center on Family Support and Children's Mental Health, Portland State University.

Mayer, K., Appelbaum, J., and Rogers, T. (2001). The evolution of the Fenway Community Health Model. *American Journal of Public Health, 91* (6), 892–94.

McPhatter, A. (1997). Cultural competence in child welfare. What is it? How do we achieve it? What happens without it? *Child Welfare, 76* (1), 255–78.

Nash, K. A. (1993). *Cultural competence: A guide for human service agencies.* Washington, D.C.: Child Welfare League of America.

Nash, K. A. (2003). *Cultural competence: A guide for human service agencies* (Rev. ed.). Washington, D.C.: Child Welfare League of America.

National Association of Social Workers. (1996). *Code of ethics.* Washington, D.C.: NASW Press.

Paniagua, F. (1998). *Assessing and treating culturally diverse clients: A practical guide* (2nd ed.). Thousand Oaks, Calif.: Sage Publications.

Patton, M. Q. (1985). Cross-cultural nongeneralizations. In M. Q. Patton (Ed.), *Culture and evaluation: New directions for program evaluation* (no. 25). San Francisco: Jossey-Bass.

Pinderhughes, E. (1995). Empowering diverse populations: Family practice in the twenty-first century. *Families in Society, 76* (3).

Rynes, S., and Rosen, B. (1995). A field survey of factors affecting the adoption and perceived success of diversity training, *Personnel Psychology, 48,* 247–70.

SenGupta, S., Hopson, R., and Thompson-Robinson, M. (2004). Cultural competence in evaluation: An overview. In M. Thompson-Robinson, R. Hopson, and S. SenGupta (Eds.), *In search of cultural competence in evaluation: Toward principles and practices* (pp. 5–19). San Francisco: Jossey-Bass.

Shipp, P., and Davison, C. (2001). Leveraging diversity: It takes a system. *Leadership in Action, 20* (6), 1–5.

Solomon, B. (1985). Seminar presentation. In S. Gray, A. Hartman, and E. Saalberg (Eds.), *Empowering the black family: A roundtable discussion with Ann Hartman, James Leigh, Jacquelynn Moffett, Elaine Pinderhughes, Barbara Solomon, and Carol Stack.* Ann Arbor, Mich.: National Child Welfare Training Center, the University of Michigan School of Social Work.

Symonette, H. (2004). Walking pathways toward becoming a culturally competent evaluator: Boundaries, borderlands, and border crossings. In M. Thompson-Robinson, R. Hopson, and S. SenGupta (Eds.) *In search of cultural competence in evaluation: Toward principles and practices* (pp. 95–109). San Francisco: Jossey-Bass.

U.S. Census Bureau. (1998). Growth in single fathers outpaces growth in single mothers, Census Bureau reports. Retrieved March 16, 2004, from www.census.gov/Press-Release/cb98-228.html.

U.S. Census Bureau. (2000). Record share of new mothers in labor force, Census Bureau reports. Retrieved March 16, 2004, from www.census.gov/Press-Release/ www/2000/cb00-175.html.

U.S. Census Bureau. (2003). Facts and features: Back to school. Retrieved March 16, 2004, from www.census.gov/Press-Release/www/2003/cb03ff-11.html.

Way, B. B., Stone, B., Schwager, M., Wagoner, D., and Bassman, R. (2002). Effectiveness of the New York State Office of Mental Health core curriculum: Direct care staff training. *Psychiatric Rehabilitation Journal, 25* (4), 398–402.

Webb, N. (2001a). Strains and challenges of culturally diverse practice. In N. Webb (ed.), *Culturally diverse parent-child and family relationships. A guide for social workers and other practitioners* (pp. 337–50). New York: Columbia University Press.

Webb, N. (Ed.) (2001b). *Culturally diverse parent-child and family relationships. A guide for social workers and other practitioners.* New York: Columbia University Press.

Wheeler, D., Walters, K., Hess, P., Franks, C., and Sheiman, E. (1999). *Self-awareness for practice in a multicultural world: A training curriculum.* Unpublished paper.

Wright, P. (Ed.). (1994.) You can use communications principles to create culturally sensitive and effective prevention materials. Technical Assistance Bulletin. Rockville, Md.: National Clearinghouse for Alcohol and Drug Information.

Chapter Four

Collaboratives

Avenues to Build Community Capacity

■ ■ ■

ANITA FLOYD

Individuals report a range of benefits from involvement in community capacity-building efforts. The following quotations highlight individual benefits reported by members of collaboratives created to support children and families and to build community capacity:

"My leadership skills have grown as well as my ability to work with diverse groups."
> —Community volunteer in a youth development partnership

"I have increased my ability to write grants, work with volunteers, and collect and report data."
> —Medical professional in a teen pregnancy prevention initiative

"[Being a part of the collaborative] has enabled me to work across racial, social and institutional boundaries in a productive way."
> —Representative from the faith community in a teen parenting partnership

"Working in this group has allowed me to broaden my 'people' skills, including networking and communicating effectively."
> —A volunteer youth participant in a youth development partnership

As a collective process for reaching common goals that cannot be achieved by individuals or organizations acting alone, collaboration is a highly valued strategy for community capacity building. However, collaboration is also a capacity-consuming process. Few collaborative groups meet all of the demanding requirements of "collaboration." If they were fully candid, those who have worked in collaboratives might be forgiven for wondering if offering collaboration as a "cure" for community incapacity isn't worse than the condition.

In general, community capacity refers to an ability to solve problems. More formally, "community capacity is the interaction of human capital, organizational resources and social capital existing within a given community that can be leveraged to solve collective problems and improve or maintain the well being of a given community. It may operate through informal social processes and/or organized effort" (Chaskin, 2001, p. 291). Community capacity can be built across formal as well as informal collaborative efforts.

In this chapter, the capacity-building role of collaboration is explored. The chapter offers formal definitions of collaboration, as well as typologies of collaborative activities. Rather than focus solely on the most highly functioning, highly collaborative community processes, the value of selecting appropriate collaborative processes for diverse community work is emphasized. The role of the coach[1] in facilitating the collaborative process is presented, along with capacity-building tasks, experiences, challenges, and lessons learned.

The chapter takes a particular look at both the capacity *requirements* and the capacity-building *benefits* of collaboration. In doing so, it draws upon experiences of the author and other volume contributors as coaches to numerous collaborative efforts.[2] The principles, lessons learned, examples, and vignettes

1. Throughout this volume, the term "coach" is used interchangeably with the term "capacity-building consultants" who provide technical assistance to community groups or organizations to support and strengthen families.

2. Through their association with the Institute for Families in Society at the University of South Carolina, the author and other contributors to this volume have served as coaches providing technical assistance to more than one hundred community groups that participated in multiyear collaborative initiatives sponsored by different foundations and federal and state governmental funders. This included provision of technical support to grantees and funders in four initiatives that required community collaboration as a prerequisite for funding. As of December 2002, IFS had completed technical assistance to the Duke Endowment for its Children and Families Program and the State of South Carolina for its First Steps to School Readiness Initiative. In September 2003, technical assistance to Communities in Schools of South Carolina concluded. Technical assistance continued through 2004 to homeless coalitions in South Carolina receiving funding from the U.S. Department of Housing and

in this chapter are based in part upon our own experiences and observations, as well as the evaluations by partnership members and project funders of their efforts in collaboration.

COLLABORATION AND COLLABORATIVE ACTIVITY

Collaboration: An Important Construct in Community Development

Collaboration in all its many forms and types is highly valued because it offers a structure for participation by community members who are affected by the community issues, along with organizations, researchers, consultants, and other stakeholders who care about these issues (e.g., Butterfoos, Goodman, and Wandersman, 1993; Chavis, 2001; Florin, Mitchell, and Stevenson, 1993; Foster-Fishman, Berkowitz, Lounsbury, Jacobson, and Allen, 2001). Collaborative efforts allow opportunity for co-learning and reciprocity of expertise, sharing of decision making, and mutual ownership of both the process and products of the collaboration (Israel, Schulz, Parker, and Becker, 1998; Viswanathan et al., 2004). The participation of community members provides an opportunity for increased contextual and cultural relevance through input to assessment and research questions, methods, approaches, etc. Collaboration is especially valued in community development efforts that address issues of disparity and in situations where an understanding of race and ethnicity is imperative. Collaboration offers an approach that builds capacity of diverse communities to take active roles (e.g., program planners, co-investigators, policy makers) in studying and addressing community concerns.

Urban Development. The initiatives have varied from those focused on particular community outcomes, such as improved readiness for kindergarten, to initiatives that have allowed the community to focus on any outcomes they identify as enhancing child or family well-being. The initiatives have varied regarding the amount of funding and the grant period, though all were multiyear. The majority of participating communities were in rural North and South Carolina. Most were working to improve a community whose geography they define. Few of the community efforts were neighborhood-based, and therefore members lacked neighborhood relations. Rather, the projects tended to focus on improving outcomes in a specific issue across a county, town, or metro area. What they had in common was the funder's expectation that the communities "collaborate" to plan, implement and evaluate their strategies. Most of these community-based collaborative efforts were developed in response to the availability of funding. In most cases, the funder contracted directly for technical assistance to the community groups. However, all local community groups funded through HUD initiated the requests for technical assistance.

Trickett and Espino (2004) provide a greatly detailed monograph on the concept of "collaboration," presenting research by feminist scholars, community psychologists, and program evaluators with the goal of "unpacking" the construct of collaboration (p. 2). They highlight collaboration as an important concept in the field of health education and community health, environmental research, organizational development, and intervention research on social issues, such as AIDS and substance abuse, and note that the concept is important in defining university-community relations. They further point to collaboration as an important concept in calls for redefining roles in school psychology, mental health services to children and families, and the physician/patient relationship. Collaboration is also highlighted in its role in varied models of participatory research and evaluation, including empowerment evaluation. The reader is encouraged to review this article for a thorough discussion on the multiple meanings of "collaboration." Trickett and Espino conclude that "more time and more stories will be useful in explicating its [collaboration's] many meanings and consequences" (p. 62). To offer more stories based upon the lengthy period of time we have been involved in collaborative activities, this chapter offers experiences that illustrate the benefits of different types of collaborative activity.

Collaboration: A Group Process with Multiple Dimensions

While there are a plethora of definitions for collaboration, it is commonly understood as a group process to reach common goals that cannot be reached through the efforts of individuals or organizations acting alone (Bruner, 1991; Mattessich and Monsey, 1992; Taylor-Powell, Rossing, and Geran, 1998). This can refer to a wide range of activities, from a short-lived task force created to plan a community celebration to a twenty-year-old neighborhood organization with a track record of housing construction, youth leadership development, and advocacy. Appreciating the value in all forms of collaborative activity is essential to "unpacking" collaboration.

TYPOLOGIES OF COLLABORATIVE ACTIVITY. To address this range of collaborative activity, the literature on collaboration, community initiatives, and coalitions offers typologies that distinguish community group efforts in a number of dimensions. These include the level and quality of interaction required from group members, goals of the effort, the structure and location of authority within the group, and the use and generation of resources. For example, Mattesich and Monsey (1992) distinguish among "cooperation," "coordination," and "collaboration." They suggest that *cooperative* relationships are informal and lack structure, planning, and common mission. In cooperative arrangements, members retain authority, resources remain separate, and benefits are limited to information sharing. *Coordination* requires more formal communication, role division, and greater planning and structure. *Collaboration* requires commitment to a common mission, comprehensive planning, and a new, common structure that determines the distribution of authority. Importantly, resources are shared or jointly pursued.

Similarly, the model developed for evaluating collaboratives by Taylor-Powell, Rossing, and Geran (1998) at the University of Wisconsin distinguishes among five collaborative processes, for which abbreviated definitions and authors' examples are provided below.

- *Communication*: This process provides a clearinghouse for information and allows members to explore common and conflicting interests, e.g., network
- *Contribution*: A process by which members informally provide each other support and resources to reach independent goals, e.g., support group
- *Coordination*: A deliberate, joint, and formalized process in which members share risk and resources to achieve complementary goals, e.g., task force, council
- *Cooperation*: A process of joint planning to achieve joint goals. Members share similar interests, e.g., partnership, coalition, consortium
- *Collaboration*: A process that requires comprehensive communication and common planning to achieve common vision. Authority is vested in the collaborative rather than individual agencies

CHOOSING THE BEST "COLLABORATIVE" FIT. Implicit or explicit in the discussions of collaboration is the higher value placed on "collaboration" versus other forms of collaborative activities (i.e., the range of collective community actions engaged in by collaboratives or partnerships). Although different collaborative strategies are developmental and can build upon one another as trust develops and issues of turf are overcome, as Himmelman (2001) emphasizes, particular strategies should not be viewed as better than others. This is an important point because a value often is placed on "collaboration" as an advanced form of group effort. For example, most academic discussion and analysis focuses on collaboration. Further, in spite of the range of typologies, little discussion focuses on the less intensive forms of interaction, even though they are probably more common. Public and private funders that require "collaboration" for funding reinforce this perspective. In our experience, it would be a mistake to understand collaboration as the "best way" to address community issues. Different strategies or collaborative activities are simply more appropriate for particular communities at a particular point in time and given their particular goals and capacities. For example, collaboration may not be necessary if improved interorganizational communication is all that is required to coordinate a community's service delivery to the homeless. Many disappointing attempts at collaboration may have been simply unnecessary from the start.

In the development of a collaborative, the coach's role supports potential partnership members as they explore the range of these collaborative activities and select from among them. In particular, guidance may be essential in helping potential members be intentional in creating structures and processes to meet their projected needs. In our experience, many partnerships either struggle to meet an expectation of collaboration that may be presented only vaguely by an entity that is funding the collaborative initiative, or they fall back on models with which they are familiar and develop their collaborative using these, for example, models of nonprofit development. As capacity-building consultants and active community members, we have observed the frustration of new partnerships that derailed due to an overemphasis on structure, in the form of, for example, protracted negotiations on by-laws or tedious applications for tax-exempt status. Conversely, others falter from a lack of attention to process, with the result that decisions are never final because a decision-making process has not been articulated.

The most effective level of structure and the type of decision making depends on the ambitions of the partnership. Early and ongoing discussions of the best collaborative fit for the goals of the group can prevent frustration. Real-life examples are a good way to make the point. For example, when coaching newly forming coalitions to serve people who are homeless, we share collaborative models that have been developed in other local communities. The models are compared regarding goals, size, resources, membership, member capacities, and even meeting structure and frequency.

The need for collaboration must also be understood as fluid. For example, changing conditions in a community may require cooperative efforts to develop collaborative capacities as the scope of an issue is explored. Conversely, the achievement of a critical outcome may provide members of the collaborative an opportunity to reduce their efforts and spend time at the less intensive activity of networking.

Vignette: From Network to Cooperation

A local, multicounty homeless coalition resisted formalizing their coalition for years. They did not incorporate, secure tax-exempt status, or even develop committees. Beyond the annual selection of leadership, the coalition had no structure. The decision to remain informal was intentional and regular. In other words, the issue was raised more than once during its first few years of operation; the group discussed the issue and decided against more structure. In spite of the informality, lack of a well-resourced lead agency, or funding to employ staff to manage the coalition, the group successfully secured nearly $8 million in HUD Supportive Housing Program funding over nine years. These funds supported individual agencies, not the coalition. Coalition members reported benefits of funding for individual agencies, as well as benefits from networking and information sharing at the monthly meetings. The workload of the coalition was significant, including data collection (e.g., counting the number of homeless people in the service area), assessing and planning how to fill service and housing gaps, and completing an annual application for the HUD SHP funds. During the first six years, the coalition's success depended on individuals volunteering to do planning and grant writing, and agency leadership being willing to serve as applicants for collaborative grants of the coalition. In the ideal world, the coalition would have assessed which agency was best positioned to administer each particular grant. Instead, the work fell to those most willing to do the work.

Today, a single agency (a relatively small nonprofit service provider) is administering three of four cross-agency grants and also coordinating data collection, analysis, and grant development for the coalition. The informal structure supported the coalition's ambitions for about six or seven years. Over the next two years, however, changes in the coalition and the environment prompted the group to restructure. The coalition had grown dramatically in active membership. Where twelve to fifteen people might have gathered at meetings in the early years, participation had grown to forty to fifty people a month. Other changes influenced the coalition's recent decision to formalize its structure. HUD requirements increased. The coalition also secured a small grant to hire a part-time staff to assist with data collection, outreach to rural counties, and other coalition activities. The

(continued)

coalition also expanded geographically to include additional counties. To accommodate these changes, the coalition added a board of directors and standing committees, incorporated, and applied for tax-exempt status. The last will allow the coalition to serve as applicant for cross-agency grants and relieve the coalition from dependency on the talent and inclination of the director from the agency that had taken on most of the coalition's work. The new structure also presents opportunities for new leadership to emerge that could enhance the long-term stability of the coalition.

Collaboration: Valuable Strategy for Community Capacity Building

The value of collaboration as a strategy for building community capacity is stressed by practitioners such as David Chavis (1997). As a process for improving a community's "control, cash and sense of community" (Chavis, 1997, p. 2), collaboration is ideal for community capacity building because collaboration is driven by relationships. Collaboration requires partners "to enhance each other's capacity for mutual benefit." The development of interventions to address specific community issues like drug abuse, inadequate housing, or school readiness represents a reason to collaborate, not the primary outcome of the collaboration. The collaboration itself is the means to community improvement.

But all collaborative efforts do not meet these criteria. Researchers distinguish between collaboratives that focus on interventions or programs and those that focus on systems change. Chavis and Florin distinguish between community-based and community-development collaboration (1990). Where service professionals direct the former by developing interventions to address community deficits, the latter is asset-focused and managed by community members. In the latter, professionals serve as resources to the collaborative, and the primary strategy is capacity building. Himmelman (2001) similarly distinguishes between collaboration for community betterment and community empowerment. These models offer different ways in which to assess collaboratives.

While distinguishing among collaborative models with regard to either purpose (betterment vs. empowerment) or intensity of interaction clarifies the range of collaborative activities, neither scheme offers much guidance regarding the community capacities to be built through collaboration. It may be clear that successful collaboration for community development or community empowerment will equip a community to determine its course, but the capacity produced (or required), for example, by networks or task forces focused on community betterment, remains relatively unexplored. Our experience with foundation and government-funded collaborative initiatives suggests that the latter are much more common than the former.

Several conditions support the inclination to pursue community betterment strategies. First, collaboratives commonly experience a tension in the focus between programming and development of the collaborative. Collaborative partners often choose to focus on programs rather than on building the capacity of members or the community. Programs and services are more tangible than skill building. Second, community collaboratives are often stimulated by a funder who invites communities to compete for funding to address a community issue. Both funders and grantees understand this to mean developing a program, providing services, or somehow meeting the needs of individuals and families in a community. Third, most grantees value the funding because it allows them to expand or improve services. This benefits the community and the agency's consumers, but agency staff also may see personal benefits from service enhancement (in terms of their own jobs). In contrast, systems change can make their work more difficult at least in the short run. This "betterment" perspective is strengthened by high participation of providers who typically receive the funding notices and often initiate these collaboratives. Thus the emphasis on services tends to diminish the focus on capacity building. In our experience, collaborative members who respond to funding availability rarely view the funding as an opportunity to build capacity for systems change in their communities, especially in the early stages of development. The membership composition of collaboratives contributes to this perspective in other ways, too. Newly forming collaboratives often are encouraged to recruit public officials and high-ranking agency administrators because of their influence and ability to commit resources to a community effort. These representatives typically support a service perspective but also tend to represent the status quo.

Funders may also diminish the capacity-building potential of collaboratives. For example, funders often expect new collaboratives to begin delivering these services within a year of funding. The short timeframe for producing programs prioritizes grantee programming at the expense of partnership development, which requires a long timeframe. An increased and widespread emphasis on outcome evaluation may have strengthened this tendency. Services are often highlighted because formal evaluation is expected regarding program outcomes but less often expected for the partnerships engaged in service development. Finally, funders who do not allow administrative or operational costs for the partnership itself deny the capacity requirements of collaboration. The Continuum of Care model required by the U.S. Department of Housing and Urban Development for Supportive Housing Program requires that local coalitions assess and plan to meet the homeless housing and service needs of their communities, but it is possible that no SHP funding will support these efforts.

It has been our experience that most collaboratives fall short of the ideal of "collaboration," with its high levels of interaction, elimination of turf issues, and free sharing of resources for community empowerment, yet these community groups do develop community capacity. In the following sections we share experiences of the communities with which we have worked, both the capacities that have been built and those that remain less developed. Later we reflect on the role of the coach in supporting capacity building.

Building Capacity Within Collaboratives

Across all the forms of collaborative activity, capacity building can occur. The collaborative process affords several means of capacity building, such as lending capacity (across organizations or to the partnership), experiential learning, modeling, securing training, or peer support.

LENDING CAPACITY. In partnerships where large organizations or high capacity organizations work with smaller ones, the larger organization can lend capacity to other organizations or to the community even where the partnership functions more as a coordinating or networking partnership.

Vignette: Lending Capacity

In a partnership created in a rural community to improve the recreational and enrichment opportunities for youth, the local healthcare system assumed the role of lead agency. While the development and supervision of after-school programs was outside the hospital's mission, its participation in the initiative lent visibility to the issues, filled a gap in leadership, and provided resources, including staff, to lead the partnership and oversee programs. Although the funding for the partnership

(continued)

required that the hospital serve as fiscal agent, there were other organizations that would have been more likely candidates to actually lead the partnership. A local college (that had the facilities the community youth coveted) and the local school district were less involved as each struggled with its own organizational issues. In the short term, the partnership secured funding for new services and redirected existing resources to improve services for youth. By the third year of the effort, the school district had succeeded in pursuing a million-dollar grant to replace and greatly expand the services initiated by the original partnership. The application for funding submitted by the school district followed from the work of the original partnership, including a resource assessment. Ultimately, partner members absorbed or secured funding to sustain the expanded services originally conceived by the partnership. The partnership again turned its focus to planning and creating a permanent facility in the community for youth recreation.

Universities also lend capacity by participating in community partnerships. Like healthcare systems, universities often represent "capacity rich" organizations, especially in small towns or in rural areas. A particular university with a poor reputation in its bordering, distressed neighborhoods facilitated a community-based collaborative initiative that funneled a variety of university resources, including students, active and retired faculty members, technical staff, equipment, and funds into the local neighborhoods.

In some partnerships, participating in a collaborative process has reshaped the way the community or participating organizations operate. Partnership members report a wide range of changes that occur as a result of their participation. Partnerships offered the community a "rallying point" for particular issues, improving coordination of services to target groups (families) and breaking down barriers among stakeholders (e.g., the faith community and public services) (Floyd et al., 2003). Members from active partnerships also report that they are more inclined to collaborate after their experience with one initiative. To illustrate, a large social service agency only tentatively offered leadership to an ambitious initiative because of fears that a high-profile role would exacerbate a community perception that it was "empire building." Yet two years later and in spite of the fact that the project was not fully realized, the organization now enjoys a reputation for collaboration and is more fully engaged in other collaborative community efforts. A former partnership member reports that the experience expanded her "collaborative horizons." In other communities, the process of collaboration, once learned, has been extended to other issues. For example, a community partnership addressing youth recreation spun off a second collaborative to address parenting issues. While the first partnership was initiated in response to a funder's request for proposals, the second partnership was community initiated. Without the promise of new funds, the parenting partnership quickly cut to the heart of turf issues and the best use of limited resources.

EXPERIENTIAL LEARNING. The premise of our capacity-building model is that people learn from doing. Thus an important and predictable benefit of participating in a partnership is that the community individuals and agencies that participate learn the skills that are being developed by the collaborative. Furthermore, through community members' participation in a partnership, capacities are developed in fundraising, especially with large development campaigns, political networking and relationship building, planning, and staff management. Community participants report developing "people" skills, including communication and networking; the ability to understand a wide range of viewpoints; facilitation skills; and effectiveness in working with a group. Other specific new skills reported include grant writing, data collection, report writing, planning, and learning to use the logic model in applications beyond the grant initiative.

MODELING. Of course, as *evaluators*, we ask partnership participants and funders to assess our performance at different points in a multiyear technical assistance contract. We incorporate both qualitative and quantitative strategies for the coaches' evaluation to reinforce the use of different methods. Modeling can be instructive for building other capacities, as well. For example, coaches can model the skills applied in facilitating meetings of collaborators or in resolving conflict.

TRAINING. Effective partnerships secure additional training to build capacity for specific purposes. For example, some partnerships have brought in development experts, especially when planning and raising funds for new facilities. Other partnerships received diversity training that influenced the mix of services they provide. A family support center recognized the growing Hispanic population in the community, secured training from a partner member, and added English as Another Language training to their services.

PEER SUPPORT. Finally, partnerships most appreciate and request peer support as a capacity-building strategy. Peer support can be accomplished in several ways. Annual conferences of grantees or providers present opportunities for informal networking. An effective process is to build peer technical assistance exercises or discussions into the agenda of partnership meetings. This can include very intentional sessions in which grantees are paired with colleagues from other programs to "problem solve" on challenges they are confronting. Conference planners also schedule sessions around topical discussions (e.g., sharing tips for writing specific federal grant applications or improving client access to specific mainstream resources) and invite participants, rather than panelists, to share their skills.

In assessments of their experience with community-based partnership initiatives, participants frequently assert their wish to avoid "reinventing the wheel." In the planning phase of initiatives, organizations' leaders and staff members often research and visit programs that are similar to those they wish to implement. Coaches can be helpful in identifying best practice programs to investigate. Coaches of large, multisite initiatives, also have the advantage of familiarity with the capacities and challenges of the different grantees. Partnership members can be referred to others for advice on particular issues.

COACHING COLLABORATIVES

Technical assistance for collaboratives varies across several dimensions. These include scope of support, individual versus team approach, "community" access, funder-grantee relationship, and capacity for collaborative activity.

Scope of Support

Coaches can be engaged to provide a wide range of services to collaboratives. These may include program planning and development, program evaluation, collaborative development or evaluation, and development and evaluation of the funding initiative. Funders typically engage coaches to provide technical assistance to grantees for both partnership and program development and evaluation of the programs, partnerships, and initiatives. There are advantages and disadvantages to this wide scope. A wide scope allows the coach better access to the "big picture." Having insights into the political conflict within a collaborative group, for example, can improve understanding of the obstacles to program implementation. Further, skills that grantees require across these areas often overlap (e.g., planning, communication, and cultural competence). The advantages of a wide scope of focus include "coach sprawl," often reflected in the expectation from grantees or funders that the coach can meet all of their needs. As an example, coaching to build capacity for program evaluation often requires additional support for program development. If the coach also is expected to help develop capacity for collaboration, sustainability, or other needs, he or she may become stretched too thin or may become so active or visible in the effort that he or she has moved from the provision of technical assistance to the role of service provider.

Individual Coach Versus Team Approach

Depending on the scope of support, coaches provide services individually or in teams. A wide scope of support permits the development of teams that include coaches with backgrounds in research and evaluation and diverse program areas (e.g., early childhood, psychology, domestic violence, community development). Preferably team members have "hands-on" experience in the nonprofit and human service delivery world. In our technical assistance to collaboratives, we have assigned a lead coach for each grantee or partnership but have also relied on the particular expertise of each coach on the team in responding to specific or unique issues of grantees or partnerships.

Example: First Steps—a Team Approach

First Steps is a comprehensive early-childhood initiative designed to ensure that all children in South Carolina start first grade ready to succeed. First Steps established local county boards to plan and implement programming according to prioritized needs in each local community (South Carolina First Steps, 2000; also see chapter 5 in this volume). All counties were required to form collaboratives to assess local needs and design interventions to address school readiness. Counties were encouraged to use science- and research-based interventions. We were hired as coaches to support both state and local efforts to assess and propose programs to impact school readiness.

(continued)

To support the local development of South Carolina's First Steps to School Readiness programs, our office provided a team of coaches. Some of the coaches were experts in evaluation and some had expertise in either partnership development or a substantive area of a program under development. Coaches supporting evaluation efforts worked directly with early-childhood development community partnerships to create process- and outcome-based evaluation plans and procedures. These coaches relied on the team members who were effective practices experts to provide advice regarding establishment of specific quality indicators and outcome measures. The effective practices experts concentrated in one of several areas defined by First Steps: child care, early education, family-strengthening programming, health care, and partnership development. The effective practices input to the coaches supporting the evaluations was critical in helping community organizations establish ways to monitor and demonstrate results.

Community

Traditionally, being a part of the "community" has been thought of in one of two ways, one focusing on place and the other on interests. Using location as the criterion, a community is defined as a group of people who live in the same geographical area (e.g., county, neighborhood, census tract). Community is also defined by individuals who do not live in the same location but share a common interest or trait (e.g., faith community, community of people with disabilities, gay community). Of course in any location, individuals associate across multiple areas of interests.

Regardless of how community is defined, the coach's connection or lack of connection to the "community" is important to the collaborative process. From a geographic perspective, when a coach works within his or her own community, she or he is more likely to have a sense of the community's assets and needs and of the local politics. On the other hand, as an outsider to this community, the coach may be able to bring a fresh perspective or ask questions or offer suggestions that insiders might not see. We have often provided technical assistance through contracts covering one or more states, so we have rarely been members of the geographical community. Our perceived neutrality as facilitators has helped grantees overcome turf battles in the early planning of initiatives and allowed us to stress difficult issues, such as diverse representation.

However, as capacity-building consultants who are also active community members, we are often members of the community of interest to which we are invited to provide technical assistance (e.g., housing for the mentally ill; after-school programs; home visiting programs for new parents). In such situations, our roles as academics or community advocates in addressing the particular community issue may have been important factors in our selection as coaches. As coaches, we acknowledge that we are not neutral on such community issues. We further acknowledge that we are advocates; we want specific community change to occur. While this lack of neutrality may be viewed by some as problematic (e.g., Stufflebeam, 2001), it fits with an empowerment approach to community change (e.g., Wandersman et al., 2004) that encourages coaches to work with programs, organizations, and communities to facilitate positive results. In whatever "community" role we find ourselves as coaches, we must continually adhere to ethical principles that guide our actions to facilitate processes and deliver products (e.g., utility, feasibility, propriety, and accuracy as defined by the Joint Committee on Standards for Educational Evaluation, 1994).

Access

As suggested in the discussion above on community, geography plays a role in the capacity-building process. The physical distance to a community site is an important factor when providing technical assistance. When working within a local community, a coach can easily participate in frequent meetings, such as monthly board meetings, or be on call for problem solving. However, if distance requires several hours of travel, the coach is more likely to schedule extended site visits with multiple contacts (board members, program staff, and other stakeholders). When distance and travel costs prohibit participation in frequent meetings, on-site support to grantees should be provided at regularly planned intervals. Coaches and collaboratives can also take advantage of technology by being in touch by e-mail, telephone, and teleconferencing.

In evaluations of technical assistance to more distant communities, consumers of our services have reported that coaches were accessible and that distance was not an obstacle to services; however, some also reported that they would have contacted the coach more frequently if she or he were located geographically closer. Differences may reflect coaching style, the developmental stage of the project, or particular needs of individual clients, all of which should be considered when defining the plan for technical assistance.

Funder-Grantee Relationship

Program officers with foundations and local government funders often establish relationships with funded partnerships and may participate in a variety of ways within them. The officer can be an important resource for a coach's understanding of a partnership and its community. To find a place in the ongoing relationship, a coach should negotiate his or her role with both the funder and the funded partnership. Even with negotiation, the coach's relationships with the partnership can suffer from real or perceived overidentification with the funder. (See chapter 6 for a fuller discussion of this issue.)

Capacity for Collaborative Activity

The capacity of partnership members to collaborate also will affect the technical assistance. Both practice and research tell us that collaboration requires a tremendous level of individual and organizational capacity to succeed. A recent analysis by Foster-Fishman and colleagues (2001) identified required critical elements of collaborative capacity across four levels: member, relational, organizational, and programmatic. Member capacities include "essential skills" both for collaboration (e.g., cooperation, communication, understanding diversity, conflict management) and for creating effective programs (e.g., program planning, design, and evaluation, and knowledge of the community and change processes). Required member capacities also include core attitudes (e.g., positive attitudes collaboration, other stakeholders, and self) and access to member capacity (through diverse membership and structures that facilitate access). The review also identifies relational capacity (requirements to build internal and external relationships); organizational capacity (ability to organize members in a productive way); and programmatic capacity (ability to design and implement meaningful programs). The list of required capacities would certainly be intimidating to a small task force trying to gather support for creating a walking path to the local school. These requirements might also prove intimidating for a statewide partnership defining strategies related to school readiness. While Foster-Fishman et al. point out that high levels of coalition capacity lead to a greater likelihood of producing desired community change, they might agree that all of the identified capacities may not be needed for all levels of community change. Our experience suggests that what is more important to community change is having the needed level of capacity for the specific goals and objectives unique to each community collaborative. Assessing the level of capacity required in a specific situation is appropriate to the role of the coach.

Effective coaches assess the capacity of the collaborative across these skills early in the capacity-building relationship. The coach works to build on the strengths of members, being careful not to overwhelm members, especially leadership, with high structure requirements, jargon, or timelines until the goals of the collaborative are clear enough to shape requirements.

Vignette: Over-Coaching

Occasionally coaches find themselves invested in the products of their collaborative efforts. Coaches almost always initiate their community-based efforts with a focus on community ownership as a core value (i.e., the community is responsible for the program development or program evaluation). The role of the coach is to facilitate the process (Fetterman, 2001); the community is to own the process. Occasionally, personal or professional interests may cause a capacity-building consultant to "over-coach."

As a member of a capacity-building team, the lead coach had an opportunity to talk with the volunteer director of a human service coalition who was giving up leadership of the coalition for personal reasons. It had been a few years since the coach had worked with the director, but the coach had enjoyed their working relationship and shared her genuine admiration for the director and the leadership she had provided in the creation of a coalition that faced many challenges. During this exchange, the director become a little emotional and confessed that through much of the early formation of the coalition, she had been intimidated by the processes, training, and technical assistance provided by the coach. Where the coach assumed that the director felt supported by the structure the coach had provided, in fact, the planning, logic models, outcome jargon, evidence-based practices, etc. had made the director feel inadequate. Upon reflection, the capacity-building consultant recognized that she had operated as if the coalition's success or failure was a measure of her own skills and competence. She had taken an ownership role rather than one of facilitation. Pressing to help a coalition that was "behind" (in terms of the funder's timetable), the coach had contributed to the director's feeling of disempowerment. The coach was reminded that "over-coaching" can inhibit, rather than engender, capacity building. Over-coaching limits capacity building.

CAPACITIES FOR COLLABORATIVE ACTIVITIES:
LESSONS LEARNED AND AFFIRMED

Many capacities are needed for successful capacity building through collaborative initiatives. The seven tasks identified in building organizational and community capacity (see the introduction and chapter 2) are discussed as they relate to collaborative initiatives. The tasks include reaching out to the community, building leadership, developing a plan for action, obtaining needed resources, building infrastructure, measuring success, and promoting sustainability. Each task *requires capacity* to achieve; however, a partnership's achievement of the tasks also *contributes to enhanced capacity* on the part of the partnership members.

This section highlights the lessons about capacity required and gained that we have learned from our experiences in coaching partnership development.

Reaching Out to the Community

A diverse, relevant, committed, and skilled membership that operates with a high level of trust is critical to successful community partnerships. A variety of factors can support or hinder the development of such partnerships. For example, particularly in rural areas and small towns, community partnerships are initiated by groups of people who have extensive personal and professional affiliations outside of the partnership. They may be members of the same church, have children in the same schools, have spouses who serve as staff or volunteers of member agencies, or share a history of being the "movers and shakers" in the community. The following are lessons we have learned about community participation.

PREEXISTING RELATIONSHIPS OFFER A SOLID FOUNDATION FOR COLLABORATION. Social and professional bonds can "jumpstart" the collaborative process. Retreating to someone's beach house to craft a proposal engenders a level of trust and familiarity that is hard to duplicate in writing the same proposal in the conference room of the local health department. Frequent member interaction allows for informal processes (discussion and decision making) that can advance progress. Multiple connections can also enhance mutual accountability.

However, there also can be drawbacks to building upon preexisting relationships. Extensive informal connections can exclude important stakeholders and complicate integration of diverse membership, particularly of consumers.

INTEGRATING CONSUMERS IN THE PROCESS. In general, integration of consumers or other program participants remains a challenge for many partnerships. Partnerships that succeed in integrating consumers use a variety of strategies. First, partnerships should make it easy for consumers to participate with creative scheduling and support. For example, partnerships working with youth should consider scheduling meetings after school. Collaboratives addressing homelessness might need to provide transportation to the meetings for people who have been or are homeless. Coaches can be helpful by cautioning collaboratives to avoid "tokenism" in recruiting and supporting consumers in the program. It can be challenging for consumers to participate as the single representative of a community or service population when the rest of the participants are providers or political decision makers.

The coach also must demonstrate flexibility. While it is easy enough for the coach to provide the partnership with suggestions for helping new participants feel comfortable with the partnership process, it requires particular creativity to develop materials and facilitate an evaluation-planning meeting when a dozen of the thirty participants are ages twelve to fourteen.

Successful partnerships also demonstrate their understanding of the value of consumers' (e.g., parents, youth, grandparents, etc.) perspective in the partnership. The parents' or youths' role is clear, and participants receive the support they require to fully participate. This may include training. To illustrate, one partnership developed a youth leadership club to help youth understand meeting processes and support their public speaking skills. Support included mentoring. In another, a young mother was tapped to represent the partnership at a meeting with the funder and felt too intimidated to go alone, so the director accompanied her (and the funder allowed two representatives to participate from that group). The same mother eventually assumed a leadership role in the partnership.

Professional service workers, business members, and public officials who participate in community partnerships can articulate what motivates them (e.g., connections with other professionals, potential funding for their agency, an interest in improving the community). The personal benefits of participation to parents or other consumers must also be clearly articulated, because the costs are at least as great. For example, one parent in a partnership we coached reported that the greatest impact on her from participating in the partnership was a growing appreciation of program needs other than those for her children. A senior citizen participant appreciated meeting well-educated people and learning Spanish. The coach can strengthen the partnership efforts to recruit parents and consumers into the partnership by reminding them to budget for consumer participant incentives or costs. As an example, one partnership covered a woman's "pet sitting" expenses to allow her to participate in a conference.

INTEGRATING DECISION MAKERS INTO THE PROCESS. In addition to knowing how to recruit and sustain members, it is important that partnerships understand whom to recruit from the community. Identifying the most relevant participants for a community partnership includes recruiting those with decision-making authority. Because so much of the success of a partnership depends on identifying and sharing resources, the people with the authority to commit resources must be included. In the words of one partnership member reflecting on the partnership's inability to secure local funds for a community center in spite of the full participation of managers of local industries throughout the program's planning, "We just never had the people who could say 'yes' at the table."

Coaches, especially if they are from outside the geographical community, should note the sources of both formal and informal leadership. While members of an executive committee may hold the leadership titles, other members of the collaborative may be more powerful when it comes to decision making. This may derive from their standing in the community, the resources they control, the role of their agency in the selected issue area, or sheer force of personality.

To ensure the participation of key people, a partnership must periodically assess its membership according to these and its own criteria. The group must clarify its strengths and gaps in skills or representation and subsequently recruit to fill the gaps identified. The coach can support the partnership in developing diverse and appropriate membership by initiating discussions of partnership needs. At different stages of development, partnerships are coached to develop the matrices of skills and community representation that the partnership requires, assess the current membership using those criteria, and brainstorm for people to fill in the gaps. These needs can change significantly. In our experience, program or service people often initiated the partnerships and invited funders or fundraisers to join later. In others, the planning process helped clarify the stakeholders, including members of particular geographic communities or neighborhoods. The community itself may change. In one community, it became clear that the partnership's effectiveness depended on the involvement of the rapidly increasing Hispanic population.

Vignette: When Are Enough Partners Enough?

It is possible to cast too large a net when recruiting partners for a new initiative. The development of a statewide initiative with a general goal of meeting the unmet needs of children stalled for several months as the group struggled to find a focus. Initiated by a small group of members from a single Protestant denomination, these conveners had a common vision for supporting academic needs of children in their state. In an effort to be inclusive, however, they invited leadership from different denominations and statewide agencies to participate in planning. They used a small planning grant to hire consultants who tried to facilitate the development of a common vision from among all of the participants. After several months of inconsistent participation and difficulty clarifying a vision from the wide array of interests, the convening group returned to their own original vision and more narrow membership. Later in the partnership development and after success in implementing programs to support children and youth in schools, the group extended invitations to some of the early partners. This broadened partnership was able to support continued program development to meet the needs of children. Many new local projects developed from this interdenominational collaboration.

Building Leadership

Like most people involved in building community partnerships, we have identified lessons related to building leadership, the second critical task in the capacity-building process. It is essential to recognize that leadership may be defined differently at different times in the process. Quality leadership is shared, sustainable, and adaptive to the needs and developmental phases of the partnership. In our experience, the first leaders in a new partnership typically are either creators or conveners. The former are charismatic leaders who inspire community members to collaborate by offering a vision of how life could be. The latter are leaders who adopt the role of facilitator.

Once a vision is developed and the group engages in the work of planning and managing an agenda, new leadership skills, those of implementation, are required. Difficulties arise when implementation is left strictly to persons who are assigned to staff the collaborative entity. The collaborative partners must continue to distinguish between programs and the partnership and should maintain a role in implementing both activities. If staff members are hired, their roles with regard to implementing programs and sustaining the effectiveness of the partnership must be clear. If not, a staff member may feel disconnected from the board or feel that the board leadership is out of touch, or the board may feel its work is done and overburden the staff. Some partnerships we worked with benefited from recruiting staff from among the original creators of the collaborative. These staff "owned" the partnership's vision and well understood the goals of the program when they initiated implementation. More typically, partnerships hire staff members who have little or no history with the partnership. These staff members require continued leadership from collaborative members. There is an equal threat when the partnership members do not sufficiently "let go" to allow the staff to make decisions, as was the case with a particular faith-based program. Staff expressed frustration that the pastors in leadership were managing the collaborative like they directed their churches—with control and authority. Staff felt the community-based work required a more consultative style and more autonomy to meet the community's needs. When leadership is unclear, the collaborative and its programs may stagnate rather than continue to develop toward its vision.

Successful partnerships build leadership and address changing leadership needs in several ways, including sharing leadership and clarifying roles. Strong partnerships develop a "core group" of leaders with a variety of skills and perspectives.

Vignette: The Right Person for Each Job

One successful partnership was developed from the vision of the "creator" leader. Once the initial planning was completed, she delegated the management of the project and the partnership to a midlevel manager in her agency. The successor had great skills in implementation (e.g., keeping records, directing staff, and managing funds). A third member of the partnership had an instinct for partnership development and often raised the necessary questions about membership (criteria and participation), authority, fundraising, decision making and other developmental issues. She also volunteered when necessary to work with others on the partnership to develop proposals to respond to the issues. A final key to successful partnership development was the program leadership provided by staff. Their competence and vision allowed the other members to fully address other issues. The high level of trust allowed this core group to share responsibilities and advance their work.

Role clarification is also important for maximizing the contribution of member resources and for preventing or addressing conflict. Members should clarify what they are able and willing to contribute to and be held accountable for those commitments. The group should also discuss authority and accountability for programs, staff, and funding. In our experience, partnerships occasionally struggle to hold agencies accountable for program outcomes and financial or program reports after funding was passed to the agency. Others struggled when staff was confused as to whom it was accountable (i.e., the lead agency, the program host agency, the coalition in general?).

When a "lead agency" facilitates a community partnership, leadership-role clarification becomes particularly critical. Funders often require that funding to a partnership be funneled through a single member, or "lead agency." Partnerships should consider an agency's mission and requirements when selecting a lead agency. To clarify, a housing authority may have the capacity to develop and manage contracts on behalf of a partnership, but its jurisdiction may be limited to a smaller geographic area than the full area serviced by the partnership. This may make it difficult for them to administer larger grants or to justify spending their funds to serve areas outside of their target. The lead agency may be asked to stretch its scope in other ways, also. For example, we have worked with hospitals and universities that coordinated after-school programs and a residential program for youth that led an effort to construct a family support center. We found that negotiation of the roles and mutual expectations of the fiscal agent and the partnership can prevent the lead agency from exerting a controlling influence on the partnership or from feeling over-exposed or liable for activities they do not control. Organizational charts and memoranda of agreement are useful tools a coach can introduce to clarify these relationships across all of these issues.

It must be recognized that building leadership is an ongoing process. Therefore, it is also important for collaboratives to create a process for developing leaders, including parent, youth, or other consumer participants. The process of developing leaders is often informal; skilled members are identified in the partnership and gradually invited to assume more responsibility. More intentional processes include the provision of training (within the partnership or by supporting the members' participation in outside training).

Developing a Plan for Action

Effective plans start with the creation of a shared community vision and partnership mission. The coach can play a key role in prompting and facilitating this discussion. In our experience, partnerships struggle less with these "big picture" activities or developing task lists and timelines than with the selection of effective strategies and developing a scope of work that is congruent with their capacity. (See chapter 5, on strategic planning for larger discussion.) For example, partnerships sometimes resisted implementation of demonstrated or research-based interventions. Others struggled to focus their services because they did not want to exclude anyone from services. This resulted in too large a service area. Particularly in rural areas, too large of a service area can quickly burn out staff.

Poor needs assessments can also undermine focus. In one four-year initiative, a particular partnership completely changed focus (from serving children with disabilities to initiating fatherhood programs) then developed at least a dozen different programs, most of which operated less than a year and reached few participants each. The staff felt stretched and dispirited. In contrast, another collaborative first focused on youth initiatives as a result of a countywide needs assessment and strategic planning process. After completing their own youth services resource assessment, the group identified middle school youth as the least served and developed programs for them while they continued to work toward their larger goal of a new recreation center. A third initiative established a clear and consistent vision and mission, adapted a national model for school support, and, with only two part-time staff, initiated more than 150 school support programs that reached thousands of children and youth in a three-year period.

A strong evaluation plan can help a partnership stay focused on the vision and mission. We use logic models (see detailed discussion in chapter 6) as a systematic way of getting program staff to articulate their program focus and criteria for success and for staying on course with that focus. While those developing the program may resist the process at first ("We thought she was trying to get us to change our program by asking all those questions"), many come to appreciate the process. As one partnership member reflected, "At first, I hated the logic model, but it is a tool that I have used beyond the grant."

Finally, a clear vision and mission can help a partnership avoid the tempting trap of changing programs to meet the needs of different funders, different local government administrators, or other key officials with authority related to the program. Coaches can assist with identifying research- or evidence-based family programs and can support collaboratives with strategic planning that includes sustainability.

Obtaining Needed Resources

The ability of a partnership to provide or obtain benefits and resources to its members is a critical capacity for success. This is complicated because underlying the creation and sharing of resources are issues of values, turf, and commitment.

Effective partnerships are skilled at assessing, contributing, generating, and distributing resources. The greatest obstacle we have observed for the partnerships we have coached is the failure of members to recognize that *the partnership itself requires resources* (time, personnel, funds) in addition to those that are required for programs or other direct service or advocacy activities. Successful partnerships directly address this issue, for example, by clarifying the value of the partnership beyond being a mechanism to funnel funds to separate agencies. This may take time. For one partnership we coached, it required two years of soul searching, but the partnership decided its role was to help members identify fruitful areas for collaboration and to support members with training and consultation. Roles were clarified in written agreements, and together the partners developed a strategy to support this specific mission. On this issue, a funder can play a key role by reviewing applications for attention to the development and sustaining of the partnership. As one partnership advised a foundation at the end of an initiative, "Devote more time to planning partnerships and facilitating collaboration. Insist resources be dedicated to organizational development."

Public funders should be equally attentive. For example, the U.S. Department of Housing and Urban Development requires local homeless coalitions (which provide continua of care) to act as planners and coordinate the application for and distribution of significant federal resources.[3] Lack of HUD funding for coalition activities, however, compromises the coalition's work and overburdens coalition members. This also limits the participation of smaller, newer, and grassroots organizations with limited capacity in favor of larger, typically public service providers or local governments.

---

3. The U.S. Department of Housing and Urban Development has required local (self-defined) communities to develop homeless continua of care in order to apply for targeted homeless assistance funds, such as the Supportive Housing Program. Coalitions convene to assess the needs for serving people who are homeless and annually review and rank applications to be submitted to HUD headquarters for funding. Though the applications are collaboratively written, the funding is awarded to individual grantees and not the coalition, and no funding is available to support the considerable planning and administrative work of the coalition. For a description of the HUD homeless continuum of care process, see http://www.hud.gov/offices/cpd/homeless/programs/index.cfm.

A successful collaborative asks its partners to contribute. The commitment of resources from across its membership is key not just for generating adequate resources but also as an expression of organizational commitment to the partnership. Successful partnerships benefit from a range of contributed resources, both funds and in-kind. In-kind resources include technical skills and support in evaluation, administrative support, data management, transportation, and facilities.

Early and consistent support from members also indicates a partnership's capacity to sustain itself and its programs or services. In externally funded initiatives, local communities are often expected to support their development. The ability and willingness of members to invest early is a clear sign of sustainability.

An early plan for sustainability is a critical component of obtaining needed resources. Almost without exception, partnerships funded through large three-year initiatives were caught off guard by the need to look for funding before their programs and goals were fully realized. In our experience, even when coaches and funders encourage early sustainability planning by providing additional training and technical assistance, the partnerships still struggle. One grantee advised, "Work on a long-term funding plan from the beginning," but partnerships are often not ready to think about sustainability. This seems especially problematic for partnerships that secure large new multiyear grants. The new resources can represent a dramatic windfall in services for the community, and, given the demands on the partnership to get a program off the ground and stable, it is not surprising that people do not immediately worry about how to replace six-figure grants in three or four years. The partnerships that are most successful in sustaining themselves are those that maintain a clear focus, document results, have a clear role for the partnership, have active contributing members and organizations, and have devoted resources to sustainability (e.g., used grant funds to secure part-time development help).

Vignette: Lead Agencies Play Pivotal Role in Sustainability

The lead agencies in well-funded collaboratives are often the most concerned partner when it comes to sustainability. They may be the most visible partner of an initiative and feel their reputation is at stake should services end for lack of funding. The lead agency may also be concerned with

(continued)

its reputation with the funder should an initiative fail. The lead agency also often takes responsibility for hiring staff for the initiative, and while the staff may be accountable to the partnership, the lead agency will deliver the pink slip if funding fails. Lead agencies respond to this in different ways. The lead agency in a multiyear, statewide initiative was concerned that it would be left with a large funding gap to fill at the end of the initiative. The partnership approached program development with the goal of creating a program that was as self-sustaining as possible to minimize the need for large new resources to sustain the project. Their strategies included increasing reliance on volunteers over time and clarifying early how much in-kind support each partner could absorb when the initial funding evaporated. In one sense, the partnership limited its reach with budgets that were smaller than what the funder might have considered. On the other hand, leadership recognized that it did not have the capacity to support fundraising activities for a large project and planned accordingly.

In contrast, a lead agency and partners may wait too long to become involved in planning with poor implications for sustainability. In a second partnership we coached, the lead agency provided the expected match to secure significant funding from a generous funder, but at a critical period of development, the partnership was led by cochairs who were not affiliated with the lead agency and who were uninvolved or were unclear of their roles. The initiative struggled for a number of other reasons, including a lack of focus exacerbated by too little direction of staff. As the time approached for the original funding to sunset, staff members were left with two strategies—engage the executive director of the lead agency or scramble for foundation money to replace the original grant. Neither strategy offered a long-term solution.

Building Infrastructure

As emphasized early in this chapter, partnerships often require a great deal of time and work. Because of the competing demands on members' time (and loyalty), it is important that partnerships efficiently manage the workload.

A partnership or collaborative requires staff. Whether staff is contributed from a member organization or hired by the partnership, staff frees the membership to work on critical issues, such as leadership development, marketing, and sustainability. Staff can be most supportive of the partnership when their roles are clear. If a staff member also manages one or more programs, he or she must have sufficient time and direction to work on partnership issues.

It is essential that the roles of staff and governing members are clear. Successful partnerships share the workload with staff. Unfortunately, the start-up of a collaborative can exhaust volunteer partnership members. This tempts them to dump partnership activities on newly hired staff. Results can range from burn out of staff to complete neglect of the partnership.

Staff turnover must be anticipated. Staff turnover can set back both program and partnership development. This is particularly costly for partnerships where members are not fully engaged in supporting the partnership.

If the collaborative has successfully engaged diverse stakeholders on a significant community issue, there will be conflict. Diverse, relevant perspectives strengthen a partnership. When managed well, conflict can contribute to healthy and successful partnership development. Conflict can be a sign that the partnership is tackling key issues, such as resource sharing or "turfism." The most successful partnerships openly experience and manage conflict in a variety of ways. Sometimes skilled leadership can work one-on-one with

---

Vignette: Destructive Cycle of Partnership Participation

We observed a staff member in one partnership reinforce a downward spiral of partnership activity. Frustrated by her perception of partnership inactivity and resenting having to organize monthly, poorly attended meetings, she stopped contacting members she thought were unlikely to show up. In the course of three years, the fifteen-member board regularly gained and lost as many as 60 percent of its members each year, making it almost impossible for partnership members to fully engage with the program or guide its direction.

---

members having the conflict. If the conflict affects the entire partnership, a neutral facilitator can help clarify issues and encourage the members to imagine solutions. The resolution is often implemented with agreements or policies adopted across the membership. From our experience, when one agency in the collaborative has been designated as the "lead agency" for funding or other purposes, partnerships typically experience conflict over the lead agency's role. Issues range from how to manage overly controlling lead agencies, to questions of accountability between member agencies and the lead agency or to whom the staff is accountable—the lead agency, the agency hosting the services or the partnership. As coaches we have served as neutral facilitators (assisting to clarify the issues and helping participants move beyond their positions to envision individual and partnership interests) and have provided resources to help the partnership resolve the conflict and implement the resolution (MOAs, organizational charts).

Conflict also surfaces over program strategies or interventions. The coach can provide research- or evidence-based information to help the partnership assess the appropriateness or feasibility of different strategies.

Measuring Success and Promoting Sustainability

Among the greatest potential benefits and challenges to members of a partnership is setting aside time and resources to learn from and build upon the experience. Time and resources must be allocated to reflect both on services provided and on the partnership. Reflection for program improvement and partnership development depends on an evaluation plan. We have found this to be among the most challenging areas of our technical assistance. While partnerships quickly develop an appreciation for the planning skills required to initiate an evaluation strategy, they experience many obstacles to fully implementing the strategy. Capacity building for program evaluation is fully explored in chapter 6. In this chapter, we highlight lessons learned from recent experience in coaching partnerships.

The resources required for evaluation are significant. Unfortunately, partnerships, especially with significant grassroots membership, do not anticipate the resources required for self-evaluation. Once underway, evaluation activities must compete for staff and partnership resources; partnership members often view this as drawing resources from programs and implicitly from clients. Some partnerships address this by incorporating external evaluators into the program budget. Others seek additional technical resources. For example, one partnership secured interns from a local university to assist with data collection and analysis. Others found resources within their partnership to support evaluation. A member agency of one partnership contributed its own evaluation staff; the lead agency in another partnership agreed to develop and manage a database for the partnership. The provision for and sharing of evaluation resources should be attended to in partnership development.

Coaching partnerships in evaluation differs from coaching individual programs in evaluation. While the partnership may have a clearly articulated mission and vision, the strategy for achieving them can include a wide range of partnership managed programs or programs sponsored by individual agencies. Developing evaluation capacity in six or seven agencies or coaching a partnership staff member to support evaluation in those agencies can stretch consulting resources. It is often difficult to anticipate the coaching resources that will be required.

Example: Scale Versus Evaluation

The problem of scale is best illustrated with a partnership that implemented a statewide initiative. The partnership's strategy of promoting local church-school partnerships was so successful that over 150 projects were initiated in three years. Each local partnership was unique; therefore, common, standardized outcome measures could not be used. Further, the local programs depended on volunteers, from whom the staff was reluctant to require "paperwork." Even though the project adopted a strategy of fully evaluating a small number of pilot sites, it was very difficult to collect outcome data.

Evaluation is only as strong as the partnership. Common obstacles to partnership development also inhibit the development of an evaluation strategy. Turfism can interfere with the adoption of effective practices if a member agency wants to hold fast to its own approach because "we have always done it that way" or if the partnership is seen as interfering with an individual member agency's internal decision making. A second and related issue is accountability. Partnerships struggle to address problems with poorly functioning members or ineffective strategies of member agencies. Evaluation sharpens the focus on effectiveness and accountability and can compel these discussions. Sometimes partnerships withdraw support for programs of these members and other times they recognize that for political or other reasons, they cannot. The partnership is left with weak programs that compromise effectiveness.

On the other hand, some partnerships have addressed the potential problem of competition simply by recognizing it and incorporating it into the planning. When members of one partnership had to adopt a child-care model for inclusion in a large family support project, the partnership leadership recognized that at least two providers would be interested in participating. The full partnership developed a vision and mission for the overall project, including outcome expectations. The partnership also fully stated expectations that agencies would sustain the programs. Child-care providers were invited to submit proposals for the child-care piece, and one of them was selected based on stated expectations. The second provider was invited to participate in other program areas that better suited its strengths.

The capacity to share evaluative information and to undertake activities to promote sustainability essentially requires partnerships to communicate. Partnerships must document their process and results and then share them with stakeholders, including but not limited to partnership members, participants, funders, and the community. Communication must be continual because the partnership depends on it for resources and participants.

The capacity to effectively communicate success and needs varies greatly across partnerships. Many partnerships with which we worked struggled early in the initiatives to write reports and submit grant proposals. To facilitate the report-writing process, a simple format is useful, for example, one that provides for grantees to update reports every six months or as required. As evaluation information becomes available, partnerships are encouraged to incorporate it into other communication, especially grant applications and marketing materials. Partnerships that are most effective in marketing the collaborative or its programs include those that budget for marketing expenses and recruit members with marketing expertise and media access (e.g., local radio or television contacts). Some programs disseminate their work nationally and statewide through conferences and workshops in which they share program curricula. A particularly successful family support program creatively responded to numerous requests for visits by organizing joint tours of its program and facilities with a nearby program with similar content. A van transported visitors from one program to another, and refreshments were served.

CONCLUSIONS

The following responses typify the community benefits reported by members of community partnerships with whom we have had the privilege of working:

> "[The partnership] raised expectations for what is possible. Brought alive a new spirit, developed some sustainable new programs, and tapped strengths in the community."
> —Higher education representative in a university-neighborhood partnership

"It [membership in the partnership] has helped me understand how collaboration can make the greatest impact upon people's lives. Working together gives you greater resources and wisdom."

—Representative from the faith community in a faith-based
neighborhood partnership

After investing the time and effort to create partnerships and programs to support children and families in their communities, these participants report benefits to themselves (increased skills and knowledge) and their communities. Particularly, these communities note positive results in developing and strengthening relations and in improving awareness of particular issues as well as specific services to community members.

Those who have participated in partnership efforts are also very willing to share that the road to collaboration is challenging. When asked what advice they would offer groups starting new partnerships, many suggested that patience, time, and an appreciation for the demands of collaboration are essential factors.

In this chapter we reviewed different approaches to the community collaborative process. While most of these collaboratives or partnerships would not be characterized as having engaged in true "collaboration," members report increased individual and community capacity as a result of their efforts. Even those in partnerships that dissolved before realizing their goals have reported benefits to the community and organizational members from participation in the collaboratives. Increased attention to the complete spectrum of collaborative activity and the community impact of different collaborative forms would improve our capacity to be more attentive to the needs and goals of our communities and to support the intentional selection of appropriate collaborative processes for our work together.

References

Bruner, C. (1991). Thinking collaboratively: Ten questions and answers to help policymakers improve children's services. Washington, D.C.: Education and Humans Services Consortium. Retrieved June 1999 from http://www.cyfernet.org/research/thinkco.html.

Butterfoos, F. D., Goodman, R. M., and Wandersman, A. (1993). Community coalitions for prevention and health promotion. *Health Education Research, 8* (3), 315–30.

Chaskin, R. J. (2001). Building community capacity: A definitional framework and case studies from a comprehensive community initiative. *Urban Affairs Review, 36* (3), 291–323.

Chavis, D. M. (1997). *It takes a just and capable village: Prevention strategies for community justice.* Retrieved December 2002 from the Association for the Study and Development of Community Web site at http://www.capablecommunity.com/pubs/Chavis031997.pdf.

Chavis, D. M. (2001). The paradoxes and promise of community coalitions. *American Journal of Community Psychology, 29* (2), 309–320.

Chavis, D. M., and Florin, P. (1990) *Community development, community participation.* San Jose, Calif.: Prevention Office, Bureau of Drug Abuse Services.

Fetterman, D.M. (2001). *Foundations of empowerment evaluation.* Thousand Oaks, Calif.: Sage.

Florin, P., Mitchell, R. E., and Stevenson, J. (1993). Identifying training and technical assistance needs in community coalitions: A developmental approach. *Health Education Research, 8* (3), 417–32.

Floyd, A. G., Andrews, A. B., Hess, P., Flerx, V. C., Rivers, J., Phillips, L., Whiting, J. A., Malson, M. R., and Kinnard, D. (2003). *Lessons learned and affirmed: The Duke Endowment Children and Families Program, final report.* Columbia, S.C.: University of South Carolina, Institute for Families in Society.

Foster-Fishman, P. G., Berkowitz, S. L., Lounsbury, D. W., Jacobson, S., and Allen, N. A. (2001). Building collaborative capacity in community coalitions: A review and integrative framework. *American Journal of Community Psychology, 29* (2), 241–61.

Himmelman, A. T. (2001). On coalitions and the transformation of power relations: Collaborative betterment and collaborative empowerment. *American Journal of Community Psychology, 29* (2), 277–84.

Israel B. A., Schulz A. J., Parker E. A., and Becker, A. B. (1998). Review of community-based research: Assessing partnership approaches to improve public health. *Annual Review of Public Health, 19,* 173–202.

Joint Committee on Standards for Educational Evaluation. (1994). *The program evaluation standards.* Thousand Oaks, Calif.: Sage.

Mattessich, P. W., and Monsey, B. R. (1992). *Collaboration: What makes it work.* St. Paul, Minn.: Amherst H. Wilder Foundation.

South Carolina First Steps to School Readiness Board of Trustees (2000). State Strategic Plan. Columbia, S.C.: Office of First Steps.

Stufflebeam D. (2001). *Evaluation models.* New Directions for Evaluation (No. 89). New York: Jossey Bass.

Taylor-Powell, E., Rossing, B., and Geran, J. (1998). *Evaluating collaboratives.* Retrieved December 2002 from the University of Wisconsin Cooperative Extension Web site at http://cf.uwex.edu/ces/pubs/pdf/G3658_8.PDF.

Trickett, E. J. and Espino, S. R. (2004). Collaboration and social inquiry: Multiple meanings of a construct and its role in creating useful and valid knowledge. *American Journal of Community Psychology, 34* (1/2), 1–69.

Viswanathan, M., Ammerman, A., Eng, E., et al. (2004, August). *Community-based participatory research: Assessing the evidence.* Summary, Evidence Report/Technology Assessment: Number 99. AHRQ Publication Number 04-E022-1. Rockville, Md.: Agency for Healthcare Research and Quality. Retrieved January 12, 2005. from the AHRQ Web site at http://www.ahrq.gov/clinic/epcsums/cbprsum.htm.

Wandersman, A., Snell-Jones, J., Lentz, B., Fetterman, D., Keener, D., Livet, M., Imm, P. S., and Flaspohler, P. (2004). The principles of empowerment evaluation. In D. Fetterman and A. Wandersman (Eds.), *Empowerment evaluation principles in practice* (pp. 27–41). New York: Guilford Press.

Chapter Five

Putting It All Together

Building Capacity for Strategic Planning

■ ■ ■

PAUL FLASPOHLER, ANGELA LEDGERWOOD,
AND ARLENE BOWERS ANDREWS

It has been said that those who fail to plan are planning to fail. Attention and forethought to envisioning the community services and supports that ensure a better future for children and families is critical given families' complex and diverse needs and the vast array of services and systems involved. In recent years, this attention and forethought has been accomplished through strategic planning activities, processes in which a coalition or organization determines where it is going over a period of time and how it is going to get there (Connell and Kubisch, 1999; Rich, Giles, and Stern, 2001).

Although it is possible for community organizations to develop a strategic plan relying solely on internal resources, leaders often find it helpful to retain a consultant to assist with the process of strategic planning. In such efforts, consultants may either provide technical assistance to the organization's staff or take a more active role and conduct the strategic planning process as an outsourced service.

Clearly, an external consultant can provide expertise that does not already exist within the organization. As discussed in earlier chapters, there are many roles a consultant might take, including providing technical assistance throughout the process or providing time-limited assistance with specific activities, such as those related to an assessment of needs and resources, facilitation of the planning process, drafting the formal strategic plan, or the implementation of the strategic plan. The role of the consultant necessarily depends on the needs of the organization, including the barriers being faced. The consultant's responsibilities should be clearly agreed upon prior to the consultant initiating work with the organization. Just as the organization must decide what is needed from a consultant, the consultant must decide if the organization is a good match based on his or her area of expertise, skill set, compatibility of values, attitude, and clarity of role. (See discussion of principles in chapter 2.) Whether the consultant's role is that of providing technical assistance or actually leading and managing the process, it is essential that he or she be very well grounded in the current thinking about strategic planning and prepared to assist the organization in assessing its readiness to initiate the process and to complete and implement a strategic plan.

In this chapter, we will define and describe strategic planning and its potential benefits, who uses it and why, some typical barriers to strategic planning and problems that can occur, elements of a strategic plan, and suggestions for engaging in effective strategic planning. Finally, we will identify some lessons we have learned about strategic planning. Throughout the chapter, we will illustrate the process of strategic planning using the South Carolina First Steps to School Readiness Initiative.

Strategic planning is a complicated but valuable process that, if implemented effectively, can help to improve the effectiveness of programs and initiatives in the human service sector. The ideas presented in this chapter will assist consultants in the strategic planning process.

WHAT IS STRATEGIC PLANNING?

Strategic planning has been defined by a variety of authors in a range of contexts and is used in many areas, including government and both the business and nonprofit sectors (Alliance for Non-profit Management, n.d.; Bryson, 1995; Deming, 1982; French, Kelly, and Harrison, 2004; Lozeau, Langley, and Denis, 2002; McNamara, 1999; Steiner, 1979; Wall and Wall, 1995; Zipke, 2003). Because there are many different definitions, theories, and processes for engaging in strategic planning, it can be very difficult for organizations and communities to figure out what strategic planning is and how best to do it.

Originally, the word *strategy* referred to the execution of military plans and reflected the traditional, hierarchical values of the military. Strategy functioned as the bridge between military plans and military tactics. In nonmilitary settings, strategy could be said to provide a bridge between an organization's goals and the organization's actions; the plan provides a unifying set of expectations so that employees and other stakeholders will understand how to work together to achieve a set of goals.

Strategic planning is one of several planned change processes that have transitioned from the for-profit business world to social service and non-profit organizations (Lozeau et al., 2002). Most models of strategic planning acknowledge that each organization should tailor the process to meet its specific needs, rather than adhere to a prescribed model. In fact, McNamara (1999) affirms that organizations develop their "own nature and model of strategic planning, often by selecting a model and modifying it as they go along in developing their own planning process" (p. 1).

Bryson (1995) defined strategic planning as a disciplined effort to produce fundamental decisions and actions that shape and guide an organization's actions. Cadwell (2002) describes it as change management that includes four steps, which, when followed, increase the likelihood of the successful implementation of the changes. These are

1. rallying people behind the change so that they understand its necessity and how it fits with their own interests,
2. designing the changes that need to occur,
3. getting stakeholders actively involved to promote ownership, and
4. implementing the changes.

We think of strategic planning as planning for change. It is a change-management process where a group of individuals within a community or organization work together to develop a roadmap for the future of the organization. Care must be taken not to confuse strategic planning with program planning (French et al., 2004). The idea of strategic planning is to develop an overarching framework, or roadmap, that examines and provides guidance regarding the interrelationships among the parts of an organization (Steiner, 1979). In other words, strategic planning is about seeing the "big picture" and the fit among the parts. Program planning is typically focused on individual areas or activities within an organization.

As a management tool, strategic planning has been used for many years in business and more recently in public sector organizations. The adoption of strategic planning and other business management tools (e.g., Total Quality Management, Deming, 1982) by public sector organizations occurred in an effort to enhance public sector efficiency, effectiveness, and legitimacy (Lozeau et al., 2002). Government bodies and accreditation agencies look favorably upon, and sometimes pressure the use of, these tools since they are seen as being "rational, modern and progressive" (Lozeau et al., 2002). Arguably, these management processes have had positive effects on businesses' capacity to obtain anticipated results; however, very little is understood about what makes strategic planning effective when it is effective.

Since the origin of strategic planning is in private-sector organizations, the process may not fit easily with public-sector organizations. It is important to indicate that coalitions and community-based organizations are not businesses and may not have an environment compatible with the intended use of these private-sector tools (Lozeau et al., 2002; Steiner, 1979). In a business, executives have authority over the action that will follow from planning. In community coalitions, action is often contingent upon voluntary cooperation rather than executive decisions; thus, strategic planning can become wishful thinking rather than a blueprint for action unless the coalition anticipates how to hold itself accountable for follow-through with the products of strategic planning.

WHAT ARE THE BENEFITS OF STRATEGIC PLANNING?

So, why should a community-based organization or community coalition engage in strategic planning? Theoretically, the strategic plan will provide a roadmap to help a group or organization to identify and answer important questions, such as where they want to go, how they are going to get there, when they want to arrive, who will do the work, and how much the process will cost. A strategic plan provides a framework for coordinating the activities of separate elements within an organization or the different members of a coalition. Rich et al. (2001) found that "comprehensive strategic planning has evolved as a process to address most of the barriers to collaboration" (p. 199). Strategic planning provides a means of eliminating barriers to collaboration. A key challenge to the success of strategic planning involves having the key stakeholders, and not merely their representatives, involved. If those involved in the process do not have the power to make decisions, little will be accomplished. Engaging in strategic planning brings both costs and benefits. In this section we discuss the potential benefits and make the case that they outweigh the potential costs.

The many and varied potential benefits of strategic planning (Alliance for Non-profit Management, n.d.; Steiner, 1979) include establishing

- a shared vision and sense of purpose among stakeholders,
- increased "buy in" to the organization and its goals,
- greater clarity of roles and responsibilities,

- improvement in the quality of services,
- a foundation for increased involvement in the organization,
- improvement in the ability to prioritize needs,
- better allocation of resources to needs,
- increased access to funders, members, and volunteers, and
- infrastructure that is more capable of addressing crises and change.

We believe a critical beneficial outcome of strategic planning is empowering the multiple stakeholders within a coalition. By engaging stakeholders across areas that will be affected, strategic planning promotes their commitment to accurate implementation of a given plan. The list of potential stakeholder-participants can include funders, nonfunding partners, service providers, associated agencies, and representatives from the community targeted by the services. The distinctions between those who "have" (e.g., those policymakers or philanthropists who provide resources such as funds) and those who "have not" (e.g. those families who are in need of the services of the coalition) should be blurred during the process of effective strategic planning. Each participant brings resources to the plan, such as knowledge, skills, effort, materials, funds, or influence. Acknowledging these various sources of power provides a basis for mutual respect and interaction among the stakeholders.

Likewise, strategic planning presents the opportunity to surface a value system that promotes trust, shared accountability, responsibility, and vision in leadership and management. Without these basic values, the strategic planning process can lose its empowering nature and become stagnant. Further developing the purpose and values of the organization will require asking and answering potentially tough questions (Steiner, 1979). However, persevering and working through these questions will often result in the development or refinement of vision and mission statements and the delineation of goals and objectives, which are vital parts of the plan. An opportunity also exists to hypothesize how to arrive at the desired future of the organization while still providing an overarching structure for the organization. This can be accomplished by articulating the purpose and mission of the organization (Steiner, 1979).

WHAT ARE THE POTENTIAL PROBLEMS AND BARRIERS TO STRATEGIC PLANNING?

Community-based organizations and other public-sector groups are under increasing pressure internally and externally to adopt private-sector tools and processes as a means of improving performance and enhancing legitimacy in the eyes of the public (Lozeau et al., 2002). Unfortunately, these management processes are not always compatible with the atmosphere of public-sector organizations. Lozeau et al. (2002) indicate that "the techniques are often promoted on the basis that they will make the organization behave more like a business.... . Yet, they are inserted into a context that is not that of a business" (p. 538). The gap between assumptions underlying a technique and the circumstances in which a technique is applied can in itself be a barrier to the process and can lead to the corruption of the technique rather than the intended transformation of the organization.

All too frequently, we have witnessed the aftermath of faulty or corrupted strategic planning in schools and community-based organizations. Glossy "strategic plan" pamphlets pulled from the rear of a file cabinet are a pretty good first indicator of a corrupted planning process or technique. A further indicator of poor planning is that very little is known about why strategic planning was undertaken, who was involved in the process, and how the plan should affect the operations or activities of the individual holding the pamphlet. This unfortunate outcome is just one example of the result of an unsuccessful process.

In this section, we will describe potential barriers to strategic planning and discuss some strategies that consultants and members of the organization can take to address or eliminate them. Being able to anticipate potential barriers will help an organization or consultant take preventative steps to avoid them. Although even the most seasoned organization or consultant will not be able to avoid every potential barrier, being able to recognize and directly confront barriers whenever they arise prevents irreparable damage to the process or the implementation of the plan.

Barriers come in many forms and can surface at any point in the strategic planning process (Bryson, 1995; Steiner, 1979; Zipke, 2003). They may be the result of previous experience with ineffective strategic planning efforts that created a negative bias among participants, from a lack of genuine buy-in from the stakeholders, or from an incompatibility between the process and the organization. Barriers may emerge to either engaging in the strategic planning process, implementing the plan, or both. General barriers may include existing hierarchies, lack of diversity in the planning group, lack of knowledge regarding the strategic planning process, or fear of change.

Barriers to Engaging in Strategic Planning

Barriers specific to engaging in the strategic planning process include the lack of time, resources, commitment, and shared vision and values. In an era of ever-shrinking budgets and ever-growing demands for services, it is difficult for organizations to justify the time and expense required to engage in strategic planning. However, as one converted stakeholder testified, alluding to the value of a good strategic plan, "How can you afford not to [engage in strategic planning]?"

As has been emphasized concerning many of the processes described in this volume, organizational readiness is essential when new initiatives are undertaken. An organization should not begin planning if it is not ready to do so. Readiness includes taking steps to secure or having previously established several commitments among stakeholders. These include commitments to long-term involvement, shared activity, shared decision making, and respectful dialogue. If these commitments are not present before the planning process begins, planning is likely to be ineffective.

Barriers to Implementing a Strategic Plan

Sometimes the process of strategic planning is successfully completed, but barriers undermine its implementation. Such barriers can lead to an implementation technique that is distorted to continue existing power roles and structures or is adopted superficially, yielding an ambiguous plan that everyone was able to agree on but has little discernable content. In such cases, the participants in the planning process may produce a document—a plan—but the plan has little meaning. They intentionally avoided, or else overlooked, one of the critical elements of planning.

It is the *process* of strategic planning, challenges and all, rather than the planning document that is produced, that lays the foundation for action (French et al., 2004; Steiner, 1979; Wall and Wall, 1995). Solid commitment to principles of effective strategic planning can help to overcome biases and get the planning group headed in a results-oriented direction. It is essential that barriers are anticipated, identified, and actively worked with rather than ignored. As is the case in many initiatives, bringing a coach[1] may aid the organization to prevent or identify and move beyond barriers to effective strategic planning. But even the presence of a coach will have little influence in making the process effective if the organization is not committed to and ready to engage in strategic planning.

1. Throughout this volume, the term "coach" is used interchangeably with the term "capacity-building consultants" who provide technical assistance to community groups or organizations to support and strengthen families.

Benefits of Planning

While the process of strategic planning is challenging and consumes time and resources, precious commodities for human-service endeavors, the benefits of planning can easily outweigh the costs. For example, by engaging the stakeholders in the strategic planning process, all persons are empowered to be more effective in their roles by making them more informed leaders, managers, and decision makers. The empowerment of stakeholders is an enduring effect that will last beyond their engagement in the strategic planning process. Additionally, if the plan is a result of sincere investment in the planning process rather than a document everyone agreed on but with little substance, it can be used as a guide for the organization. Although revisions to the planning document will be necessary, the goals, objectives, vision, and mission statements can serve as tools to support the organization's leadership in effectively and efficiently managing the organization as it moves into the future.

AN EXAMPLE OF STRATEGIC PLANNING

To provide a real life example, throughout this chapter we will examine the process of strategic planning in the South Carolina First Steps to School Readiness Initiative (Section 59-152-10, 20, 30 South Carolina Enabling Legislation, approved June 28, 1999). This is a statewide legislative program that established public-private partnerships in each of South Carolina's forty-six counties for the purpose of mobilizing citizen action to assure that each child in the state is ready for school. First Steps is essentially a collaborative initiative on several levels: state, county, local services, and child and family. The overarching idea is to transform community systems so that future change, not just immediate needs, can be effectively managed.

Within the First Steps Initiative, both state and regional strategic planning were conducted with explicit attention to each of the multiple determinants of school readiness (health care, quality child care, early education, and family strengthening) and the interrelationships among them. The state strategic plan provided a vision for developing and supporting the multiple domains of early childhood development across the state. Likewise, each county was charged with developing a comprehensive strategic plan for addressing multiple domains in order to promote the goal of every child entering school ready to succeed. Strategic planning in each county used a two-stage grant process that closely mirrored the ten accountability questions that form the basis of "Getting to Outcomes" (Chinman, Imm, and Wandersman, 2004; Wandersman, Imm, Chinman, and Kaftarian, 2000). The GTO strategies for comprehensive quality programming are designed to promote effective self-evaluation through systematic planning, implementation, and evaluation of programs and initiatives. Counties applied for and received planning grants to assess their needs and resources (step one), developed goals and objectives related to priority gaps between needs and resources (step two), and initiated a strategic planning process toward improving school readiness. Upon development of their strategic plans, county boards applied for implementation grants to improve services that promoted school readiness.

Vignette: Building Board Capacities in SC First Steps County Partnerships

The South Carolina First Steps initiative takes a novel approach to policy and program development for school readiness by mobilizing comprehensive community-based action on behalf of young children and their families. The fundamental theory of change behind this approach is that local citizens, acting together though participative democratic processes can create sustainable change in community interactions and infrastructure in ways that enhance child well-being and school readiness. Further, the initiative builds upon the beliefs that

- many resources for early-childhood development exist;
- the amount and type of resources vary from one community to another;
- in all communities, certain gaps in resources exist;
- each community needs a unique plan to fill its gaps by building on its resources;
- implementation of the plan must involve coordination of existing and new resources;
- families, as their children's primary caregivers, need help from the community in mobilizing and coordinating the appropriate resources for their children.

(continued)

While there is a State Office of First Steps and a state board, the primary work of First Steps occurs through the leadership of forty-six local county partnership boards that cover the entire state. Once established, the initial charge of each board was to conduct needs and resource assessments and build a strategic plan based on the findings from these assessments. To ensure that all county partnership boards had effective leadership skills to accomplish this essential task, technical assistance was provided to each. Board members for each of these partnerships were drawn from a wide array of sectors and backgrounds. Among those included were experts in the field of early childhood and family education; parents of children eligible for services through the First Steps program; local school district and state agency officials; child care providers and advocates; and members of the faith and business communities. In addition to the representation of multiple sectors and fields, the partnership boards were diverse in terms of gender, race, and ethnicity. Thus, board members came with varying levels of skills and capacities needed to carry out their responsibilities. Coaching provided to county partnerships facilitated skill development in the following areas:

- board governance (i.e., adherence to nonprofit corporation laws and regulations, board responsibilities, and process management);
- planning (including needs and resource assessment and strategic decision making about effective early-child development programs and practices);
- grant making (including procurement, decision making about allocation of state funds, contract development, and fiscal accountability);
- evaluation; and
- collaboration (e.g., inclusive community participation and interagency relations).

These supports were provided in three primary modalities:

1. Coaching
   - On-site by the staff of the State Office of First Steps
   - On-site by the PIE (Planning-Implementation-Evaluation) team
   - Fiscal assistance by State Office of First Steps

(continued)

2. Statewide training through leadership summits (a wide range of topics from organizational development, board management, to effective practices research)
3. On-site board development training provided by nonprofit organizational development specialists

Additionally, First Steps also facilitated program-specific planning for each determinant of school readiness through the Planning-Implementation-Evaluation system (Flaspohler et al., 2003; Wandersman et al., 2003). The PIE accountability system consisted of tools and processes to promote effective self-evaluation of each program in every county of the statewide initiative. For example, within the healthcare strategy, program plans were developed for such efforts as early home-health visiting and childcare center-based health screenings and referrals to medical homes. PIE tools and processes were used to plan, implement, and evaluate the individual components (programs or initiatives) of each county's strategic plan. The evaluation of county and state strategic plans is conducted through an annual assessment process by the state office and a three-year external evaluation.

WHAT DOES AN EFFECTIVE STRATEGIC PLANNING PROCESS ENTAIL?

Although the process of strategic planning is somewhat standardized, it should still be expected to look different in each organization. This section focuses on the facets of strategic planning commonly found across organizations, including a practical plan, stakeholder commitment, and a focus on the process. It concludes with the five general steps organizations typically follow as they move through the strategic planning process.

There are five stages to a strategic planning cycle: (1) getting ready, (2) articulating purpose, (3) taking stock, (4) developing strategies, and (5) reviewing the process and outcomes (see figure 5.1).

Getting Ready

The first step in developing a strategic plan for any organization should be "getting ready" or "planning to plan." Because the process often requires a new relationship among a set of stakeholders, it is valuable to begin by defining

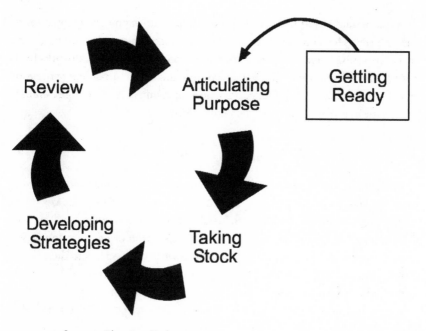

FIGURE 5.1: Strategic Planning Cycle

a set of common expectations about the way that a group will move forward with the process. In this phase, consultants can assist the organization in setting ground rules for communication and conflict resolution. In planning to plan and throughout the process, consultants should address the value and worth of joint strategic planning, the roles and value of participation of specific key stakeholders, and the steps and procedures that will be followed during the process.

In this initial phase it is also important to identify a framework for doing strategic planning that fits the organization or coalition. When choosing a framework, it is necessary to consider whether the planning will be issue based or goal based, whether a consultant will be retained or a staff member will lead the process, how a consultant might be used (e.g., to offer consultation; to provide technical assistance, including serving as a coach; or to provide service), and which stakeholders should be involved and what their roles will be. When a coach to the strategic planning process is retained, it is critical that the coach and the organizational authority or authorities retaining the coach determine which planning framework will be used. There are a number of strategic planning frameworks available, including "Getting to Outcomes" (Wandersman et al., 2000), "Precede-Proceed" (Green and Kreuter, 2004), "Communities That Care" (Hawkins and Catalano, 1992), and the "Search

Institute Assets Model" (Benson, 1997). A strategic planning framework provides the basis for a common language and set of common expectations among stakeholders. Greater continuity between strategic planning frameworks (e.g., GTO) and program planning frameworks (e.g., PIE) both simplify the process for participants and reduce instances of confusion that might emerge from products (e.g., plans and data-collection expectations).

Articulating the Purpose

This second phase of planning involves developing or refining vision and mission statements, stating the guiding principles, and articulating the organization's values. Some of the topics that the coach and participants will need to explore in the process include the reasons the coalition or organization exists, what it should be trying to accomplish, and what will constitute the organization's success. The question "Who are we?" must be answered in specific terms, which will then help to guide the organization in making decisions on how it will conduct itself and under what values it wishes to operate.

Taking Stock

Assessing the organization's current situation is the third phase. In this process, the broad question to be answered is "Where are we now?" To answer this, the coach and participants should identify both internal and external factors that could either aid or hinder the group's efforts. This might be accomplished via surveys of the staff, opinion polls in the community, or other data collected from other sources. Performing a SWOT (strengths, weaknesses, opportunities, and threats) analysis can be a useful mechanism for assessing the internal and external perceptions of the organization, which is an important part of knowing where the organization is now. Through this analysis of the organization's strengths, weaknesses, opportunities, and threats, potential strategies can be identified. This will involve extensive data collection that can then spark discussions amongst the stakeholders and hopefully lead to the clarification of the planning priorities (Alliance for Non-profit Management, n.d.).

Developing Strategies

Once the priorities have been set, the questions of "Where do we want to go?" and "How do we want to get there?" will be addressed during the fourth phase. This phase focuses on the construction of the strategic plan, which will then serve as a roadmap for the organization. As previously discussed, the goals and objectives of the organization will need to be established or revised. Project work plans or action plans, financial plans, communication plans, and evaluation plans should all be developed.

Review

In the final phase, evaluation of the organization's progress towards its stated goals and objectives takes place. The nature and extent of this evaluation will depend on the organization and the targets to be assessed. In this phase, the coach assists the participants in the process in answering the question "How are we doing?" The answers to this question then naturally lead into a review and possible revision of the strategic plan.

Discussion of the five stages of strategic planning leads to contemplation of how long the process should take. We posit that strategic planning should be considered a continuous rather than discrete activity. There is no limited time frame in which strategic planning must occur. Because strategic planning involves medium- to long-term plans, it can be thought to occur over years. So the logical next question is, how does one know when the process is completed? In reality, the process should never end but rather be an iterative one. As figure 5.1 shows, strategic planning is a circular process, with review being an integral aspect. The plan should be reviewed and adjusted periodically, resulting in a continually evolving plan.

The process and the outcomes of strategic planning will look slightly different in each community organization, but the five previously discussed steps are generally engaged in when successful planning occurs. Omitting any of the steps will weaken the strategic planning process, limit the benefits it brings to the organization, and potentially create more barriers. No one step is any more important than the others, but some may be less challenging or require less time than others. These steps can be used as a general model to guide the process of strategic planning for an organization.

The process of strategic planning, and its resulting plan, should make sense and be logical and manageable. The plan should be of a scope that is feasible with the time and resources available to the organization. Simultaneously, a strategic plan should be detailed and should reflect what is really intended to happen. This means that the plan should not be an embodiment of the unattainable ideal for the organization, nor should it be so general that no one can determine when the plan has been completed (Zipke, 2003).

Additionally, the plan derived from the process should be perceived as a medium- to long-term one and likely will not result in immediate changes. Strategic planning is about developing a roadmap for the future of the organization, not a plan to accomplish tomorrow. In addition, care must be taken not to confuse objectives or tactics with strategy. If the plan is designed to have short-term results, then it is most likely an operational plan rather than a strategic one (French et al., 2004).

The idea that strategic planning should require a commitment on the part of the employees or stakeholders is an important but often overlooked aspect of the process, with attention instead being paid to the plan's technical aspects. If the plan does not require some type of commitment, the likelihood of implementation will decrease (Rossy, Glassman, and Dahl, 2000) and the likelihood of multiple barriers will increase.

As previously mentioned, the process of developing a strategic plan will be slightly different for every organization. The size of the organization, the nature and number of the people involved in the planning, and the organization's focus all will influence the process. For example, a large organization will have more stakeholders to include than a smaller one. Also, whether the organization is for-profit or not-for-profit will affect the focus of the planning (McNamara, 1999).

Planning is most effective when the boundary between planning and implementation is blurred. It should be a process-focused activity that includes ongoing assessment and the flexibility to amend the plan when necessary (Steiner, 1979; Wall and Wall, 1995). This means that the creation of a formal document will not signify the end of the planning process. Instead, the evaluation results will have the potential to shape the plan, resulting in a link between the development and implementation portions.

WHAT ARE THE PRODUCTS OR OUTCOMES OF STRATEGIC PLANNING?

The development of a specific plan is the obvious intended outcome of a strategic planning process. Often, the product of effective strategic planning is a set of integrated documents that are consistent with the broader mission and vision of the organization. Although there is no standard format for the documents that make up the strategic plan, they should identify the key people, activities, timelines, resources, target groups, and evaluation plans for a given project (McNamara, 1999; Steiner, 1979). The articulation of vision and mission statements, goals and objectives, project work plans, financial plans, communication plans, and evaluation plans are often outcomes of this process. In this section we will discuss these documents and define their content, using examples from First Steps for illustration. If strategic planning is a roadmap for the organization, then the plan can be thought of as outlining the route that will be taken.

The typical elements or products of strategic planning are the following (Alliance for Non-profit Management, n.d.; Steiner, 1979):

- Vision: Describes a future destination
- Mission: Tells why a group exists and how it seeks to benefit society
- Goals: Long-term statements
- Objectives: Short-term targets to help reach goals
- Project Work Plans: States what needs to be done to meet each objective
- Financial Plans: Links the strategic plan to the budget
- Communication Plans: How to get the organization's message out
- Evaluation Plans: How and when progress toward goals and objectives will be measured

Vision and mission statements do not have a standard form, but typically the vision statement is broader than the mission statement. The vision statement will describe what success would look like, built upon reasonable assumptions about the future. A mission statement will include the goals of the organization, the people that the organization serves, and things that make the group distinctive.

For example, the vision statement of First Steps is general: "Every child in South Carolina will arrive at first grade ready to succeed." The mission statement of First Steps is more specific:

First Steps will promote improved school readiness through collaborative state and county partnerships that generate results-oriented initiatives. First Steps initiatives will mobilize communities to (a) enhance the readiness of young children to enter first grade successfully in terms of cognition, general knowledge, language, health, social skills, and emotional well-being; (b) strengthen the capacity of families to be their children's first and most important teachers; and (c) facilitate integrated service delivery.

(SC First Steps to School Readiness Board of Trustees, 2000)

The program goals and objectives are closely related and follow from what is articulated in the vision and mission statements. Objectives are short-term targets that when reached aid in the attainment of the goals. They need to be concrete, measurable, and realistic aims. While a goal may have one or more related objectives, care must be taken that the goals are related to the everyday activities of the organization and are not grandiose (Fetterman, 1996). These goals and objectives can then serve as a guide for developing operational plans and as a reference for evaluation. The goals articulated by First Steps are as follows:

- Provide parents with access to the support they might seek and want to strengthen their families and to promote the optimal development of their preschool children;
- Increase comprehensive services so children have reduced risk for major physical, developmental, and learning problems;
- Promote high-quality preschool programs that provide a healthy environment that will promote normal growth and development;
- Provide services so all children receive the protection, nutrition, and health care needed to thrive in the early years of life so they arrive at school ready to learn; and
- Mobilize communities to focus efforts on providing enhanced services to support families and their young children so as to enable every child to reach school healthy and ready to learn.

(SC First Steps to School Readiness Board of Trustees, 2000)

The six key objectives of First Steps are as follows:

- First Steps county initiatives will support quality, non-duplicative and integrated community-based programs that are relevant and accessible to young children and their families.
- First Steps will develop a statewide system to assess how First Steps is enhancing children's progress toward school readiness.
- First Steps county programs will be designed and continuously improved in accordance with emerging knowledge about effective practices for promoting school readiness of young children prior to first grade.
- The First Steps initiative will operate according to high standards of accountability.
- The State Board and Office of First Steps will provide quality leadership and support to ensure that First Steps initiatives are well coordinated and effective across the state.
- The State Office of First Steps, in conjunction with the Strategic Planning and Administration Committee of the State Board, will develop

an Implementation Plan with benchmarks and annual objectives to monitor progress toward the strategic goals in this plan.

(SC First Steps to School Readiness Board of Trustees, 2000).

The project work plan can also be thought of as the plan for action. It outlines what needs to be done in order to meet each objective. It is a practical guide that should include an identification of the key people, when each activity will start and end, and the resources that will be needed.

The bridge between the strategic plan and the budget is the financial plan. This should be based on the identified goals and objectives and address such concerns as revenue and expenses, for both the short and long term. But a financial plan is not the same thing as the organization's budget. It will inform those making the financial decisions of the organization about the financial aspect of the strategic planning process and will ideally help guide the organization's development of financial resources and allocation of funds.

First and foremost, a communication plan will include a decision on if a communication strategy is needed for the organization. If so, it will then typically identify the target audience, the message, and how the message should be communicated. The activities carried out with the execution of this plan will be a type of marketing.

The frequency and manner of assessing the organization's progress toward reaching its goals and objectives will be outlined in an evaluation plan. There are a variety of methods of evaluating progress, including the use of focus groups, surveys, and observation. Careful consideration should be given to choose the method that will best determine the amount of progress that has been made, rather than choosing the easiest or quickest way. These periodic evaluations can then be used to make adjustments in the strategic plan.

The tangible result of strategic planning, the plan, typically includes eight parts: vision statement, mission statement, goals, objectives, action plan, financial plan, communication plan, and evaluation plan. Although some organizations may question if all eight parts are necessary, we suggest they are. It must be remembered that strategic planning is a process first and foremost, which means that the value of the plan will be found more in the process that developed each section and less in the actual document.

CONCLUSIONS

Effective strategic planning requires integration with other organizational development processes (e.g. operational planning, evaluation). Strategic planning is a structure that links the array of elements or processes within an organization. Developing, observing, and learning from the structure helps to promote understanding of the relationships among these processes and the various elements of the organization. Effective strategic planning is not an in-depth look at a particular unit, nor is it an expansive overview of the organization that does not touch the units. Rather, effective strategic planning looks at both the parts *and* the whole of an organization simultaneously in an attempt to help figure out what the organization is doing, how it is doing it, and how it can be done more effectively.

The process of strategic planning should also not be anticipated to be as smooth as it appears to be on paper. Like any other aspect of growth and change, it is a human endeavor and is subject to all of the same dynamics and idiosyncrasies one would expect when more than one person is involved in making decisions (and determining allocation of resources). In short, strategic planning can be a politically and psychologically charged process. In our experience, we have found it useful to anticipate bumps and barriers from the beginning, acknowledge this at the outset and work collaboratively to address barriers before they arise, and promote transparency within the process. Indeed, we have found that the challenge of politics and dynamics in the strategic planning process can become an opportunity for the group or organization. In the role of coach, we have often found that the strategic planning process becomes an opportunity for groups and organizations to surface conflicts and address them collaboratively.

In the human service sector, strategic planning should be collaborative and participatory. Key stakeholders who represent all facets of the organization should be invited to be active participants. The human (psychological) factors that underlie effective change management must be attended to in order to promote the process. This means that the stakeholders must explore ideas such as understanding why change is necessary and how it will benefit those who will be involved in change.

Finally, effective strategic planning in any sector should be malleable and developmental. Plans should be reviewed and revised on a regular basis in accord with the best available information at any given time. When information or data suggests that plans are no longer manageable, successful, or aligned with current needs, strategic plans should be revised. Likewise, the creation of the plan should not signify the end of the process, and revision should not be put off until the plan is obsolete. To be successful, strategic planning should be embraced as a cyclical process that is never finished, nor complete.

References

Alliance for Nonprofit Management. (n.d.). Strategic planning. Retrieved January 2, 2005, from http://www.allianceonline.org/FAQ/strategic_planning.

Benson, P. (1997). *All kids are our kids: What communities must do to raise caring and responsible children and adolescents.* San Francisco: Jossey-Bass.

Bryson, J. M. (1995). *Strategic planning for public and nonprofit organizations* (Rev. ed.). San Francisco: Jossey-Bass.

Cadwell, R. (2002). Four key steps in change management. *Decision, 3,* 10.

Chinman, M. J., Imm, P. S., and Wandersman, A. (2004). *Getting to outcomes 2004: Promoting accountability through methods and tools for planning, implementation, and evaluation.* Santa Monica, Calif.: RAND Corporation.

Connell, C. M., and Kubisch, A. C. (1999). Applying a theory of change approach to the evaluation of comprehensive community initiatives: Progress, prospects, and problems. In C. M. Connell, A. C. Kubisch, L. B. Schorr, and C. H. Weiss (Eds.), *New approaches to evaluating community initiatives. Vol. 1: Concepts, Methods, and Contexts.* Washington, D.C.: The Aspen Institute.

Deming, W. E. (1982). *Out of the crisis.* Cambridge, Mass.: MIT.

Fetterman, D. M. (1996). Empowerment evaluation: An introduction to theory and practice. In D. M. Fetterman, S. J. Kaftarian and A. Wandersman (Eds.), *Empowerment evaluation: Knowledge and tools for self-assessment and accountability* (pp. 3–46). Thousand Oaks, Calif.: Sage Publications.

Flaspohler, P., Wandersman, A., Keener, D., Maxwell, K. N., Ace, A., Andrews, A. B., et al. (2003). Promoting program success and fulfilling accountability requirements in a statewide community-based initiative: Challenges, progress, and lessons learned. *Journal of Prevention and Intervention in the Community, 26* (2), 37–52.

French, S. J., Kelly, S. J., and Harrison, J. L. (2004). The role of strategic planning in the performance of small, professional service firms: A research note. *Journal of Management Development, 23* (8), 765–76.

Green, L. W., and Kreuter, M. W. (2004). *Health promotion planning: An educational and ecological approach.* San Francisco: McGraw-Hill.

Hawkins, D. J., and Catalano, R. F. (1992). *Communities that care.* San Francisco: Jossey-Bass.

Lozeau, D., Langley, A., and Denis, J. L. (2002). The corruption of managerial techniques by organizations. *Human Relations, 55* (5), 537–64.

McNamara, C. (1999). Basic overview of various strategic planning models. *Strategic Planning (in nonprofit and for-profit organizations).* Retrieved January 2, 2005, from www.mapnp.org/library/plan_dec/str_plan.htm.

Rich, M. J., Giles, M. W., and Stern, E. (2001). Collaborating to reduce poverty: Views from city halls and community-based organizations. *Urban Affairs Review, 27* (2), 184–204.

Rossy, G. L., Glassman, A. M., and Dahl, J. G. (2000). Tailored management development as a vehicle for strategy implementation. In R. T. Golembiewski (Ed.), *Handbook of organizational consultation* (2nd ed., pp. 881–91). New York: Marcel Dekker.

South Carolina First Steps to School Readiness Board of Trustees (2000). State Strategic Plan. Columbia, S.C.: Office of First Steps.

Steiner, G. A. (1979). *Strategic planning: What every manager must know.* New York: The Free Press.

Wall, S. J., and Wall, S. R. (1995, Autumn). The evolution (not death) of strategy. *Organizational Dynamics,* pp. 6–19.

Wandersman, A., Flaspohler, P., Ace, A., Ford, L., Imm, P. S., Chinman, M. J., et al. (2003). Pie à la mode: Mainstreaming evaluation and accountability in each program in every county of a statewide school readiness initiative. *New Directions for Evaluation, 99,* 33–49.

Wandersman, A., Imm, P. S., Chinman, M. J., and Kaftarian, S. (2000). Getting to outcomes: A results-based approach to accountability. *Evaluation and Program Planning, 23* (3), 389–95.

Zipke, A. (2003). Strategic planning by choice not by chance. *International Journal of Reality Therapy, 23* (1), 24–26.

Chapter Six

Building Capacity for Self-Evaluation Among Community Agencies and Organizations

■ ■ ■

VICKI CROCKER FLERX

Until recently, family service agencies and organizations operated under an assumption of success. The culture of helping agencies and professionals included the belief that human service delivery is an "art," not a "science," and that the results of such services are too abstract and intangible to be assessed in any systematic way. During the past two decades, however, the need for family services has been increasing rapidly at the same time that private and public resources to support these services have become scarce. This increased demand for scarce funds has resulted in a heightened expectation among both public and private funders, including foundations, that human services programs be accountable and demonstrate their effectiveness. In response to this expectation, many programs and agencies have either contracted with outside evaluation professionals or attempted to incorporate program evaluation into their own operating procedures. However, outside contracts stretch already tight budgets, and the capacity to plan and conduct an internal evaluation, particularly outcome evaluation, still lies outside the capabilities of staff and administrators of many programs.

Due to the difficulty that many family service programs experience in meeting increased expectations of accountability and effectiveness, some private foundations and other funders have begun providing resources to build evaluation capacity within an agency or program as part of the funding process. One way to help programs build capacity for evaluation is to fund consultants to support the evaluation efforts of the grantees, stipulating that the agency and program staff members work with the consultant to evaluate the newly funded program. There are several benefits to increasing the capacity of an agency to perform self-evaluation. First, program staff members who are able to conduct their own evaluation can use their data for continuous program improvement and can usually plan and implement an evaluation for future programs. In addition, increased capacity for self-evaluation helps agency administrators and staff members become better consumers of external evaluators' services and of evaluation results.

This chapter presents a model of technical assistance for practitioners who work with community-based agencies and organizations to increase capacity for program self-evaluation. The chapter describes the theoretical framework for this model, provides illustrative vignettes, and delineates several important lessons we have learned in our own work. Also, step-by-step details for technical assistance in support of building self-evaluation capacity are offered.

The model for building self-evaluation capacity presented here is not suited to all situations where program evaluation is needed. Agency administrators and staff, as well as external funders, must share the goal of developing the organization's or community's capacity for program evaluation. Further, they must understand the process by which evaluation capacity is built and be willing to wait patiently for evaluation results, particularly those related to outcomes. Therefore, in many instances, a more traditional external evaluation is a better method for determining the success of a program. The first and most important task for a coach or capacity-building consultant[1] is to help a program or funder decide if this approach to program evaluation is a wise choice.

APPROACH TO SELF-EVALUATION

Giving Evaluation Away: An Attitudinal Shift for Consultants and Participants

Program evaluation is complex and affected by numerous stakeholder and program factors. Efforts to demystify program evaluation and prepare program

---

1. Throughout this volume, the term "coach" is used interchangeably with the term "capacity-building consultants" who provide technical assistance to community groups or organizations to support and strengthen families.

staff to conduct self-evaluation involve a process of "giving evaluation away," a term used by Stevenson, Mitchell, and Florin, (1996) and further discussed by Andrews, Motes, Floyd, Flerx, and Lòpez-De Fede (2005). It is a process of sharing expertise and control that differs from the way in which external evaluators usually operate. Therefore, building capacity for program self-evaluation may require a fundamental attitudinal shift on the part of the coach that represents one of the most important differences between conducting an external evaluation and building a program's capacity for self-evaluation. In order to help an agency or organization develop evaluation capacity, the capacity-building consultant must relinquish expertise and control, thus, "giving evaluation away." This is often quite challenging for those whose training and experience is in the field of traditional evaluation. To be successful at evaluation capacity building, a coach must accept that the responsibility for program evaluation lies with those who are intimately involved in program planning and implementation, rather than with the "evaluation expert" (Stevenson, Mitchell, and Florin, 1996). Program and agency participants may also need to shift attitudes if the capacity-building effort is to succeed. The capacity-building consultant must help participants believe that they can conduct program evaluation. In addition, participants may need to change their expectations concerning who carries out the work of evaluation and who ultimately is responsible for completing the evaluation. Finally, it is important for the participants to realize that the evaluation results will help them improve their program and move them toward positive program outcomes.

Role of the Coach

An important difference between external evaluation and self-evaluation involves the role of a coach facilitating self-evaluation as compared to that of an external evaluator. The capacity-building consultant, here referred to as a "coach," typically provides technical assistance. In reality, however, the role is multifaceted, including that of "expert," teacher, conflict manager, mentor, and source of emotional support (Fetterman, 2001). Although the stated goal of the coach is to build organizational capacity for self-evaluation, in practice, coaches supporting self-evaluation usually also spend significant time providing technical assistance regarding program development and implementation. Since a good evaluation is inextricably linked to a clear, theoretically sound program plan, a coach often must spend considerable time helping the evaluation team (i.e., community members ultimately responsible for the evaluation) clarify the program goals and objectives. In addition, the team may need to define the target population more specifically and assess the program's theory of change. Coaches often must support team members who fear failure at learning evaluation tasks, help resolve staff conflict that interferes with the capacity-building process, and teach the team how to develop effective forms and data-collection procedures.

Theoretical Framework

Multiple evaluation approaches are important contributors to organizational capacity building (Campobasso and Davis, 2001; Fetterman, Kaftarian, and Wandersman, 1996; Hernandez and Visher, 2001). Capacity-building consultants need a thorough understanding of the theory, knowledge, values, and skills associated with traditional, external program evaluation (e.g., research methodologies, including qualitative and quantitative methods; experimental and quasi-experimental research designs, and implications of such issues as ethics, politics, organizational management on evaluation) (Ginsberg, 2001; Weiss and Jacob, 1988), as important prerequisites for those interested in building organizational capacity for evaluation. Further, the program evaluation standards developed by the Joint Committee on Standards for Educational Evaluation (1994) are essential to both external and self-evaluation efforts. These standards call attention to the need for evaluation strategies that emphasize utility (meeting the needs of the intended users); feasibility (conducting realistic, practical, and cost-effective studies); propriety (attending to ethical issues, especially human subjects); and accuracy (gathering and reporting reliable and valid data).

In addition to general knowledge and principles related to program evaluation, it is imperative that the capacity-building consultant or coach be knowledgeable of the theoretical frameworks of the growing numbers of participatory models of program evaluation. These models, developed from a range of disciplines, including sociology, psychology, organizational development, and education, are defined by a range of names, including empowerment evaluation (Fetterman, 1994; Fetterman, Kaftarian, and Wandersman, 1996; Fetterman and Wandersman, 2004; Garvin, 1994; Linney and Wandersman, 1991), participatory research, action research, participatory action research, and participatory evaluation (Brown and Tandon 1983; Brunner and Guzman 1989; Grundy, 1986; Kemmis and McTaggart, 1988; Whyte, Greenwood, and Lazes, 1991). Although these theory-based models of program self-evaluation are described in the professional literature as discrete models, in practice the theories and skills often blend and overlap, especially regarding the engagement and participation of stakeholders in the process of evaluation.

Our approach to self-evaluation, largely built upon the principles and traditions of empowerment evaluation, integrates program evaluation with social change processes. It articulates a strong belief in individual and collective empowerment. Organizations and communities realize collective empowerment through active, inclusive participation in group decision making, social responsibility, mutual support among participants, and group capacity building (Andrews, Guadalupe, and Bolden, 2002; Israel, Checkoway, Schulz, and Zimmerman, 1994). To be empowered as a group, an organization or a community needs the ability to plan, enact, and evaluate interventions that matter to the group or the community (Andrews et al., 2005). To be empowered is to attend to personal, social, economic, and political factors with a goal of facilitating action that will improve participants, organizations, and communities.

The empowerment evaluation process is essentially democratic, collaborative, and developmental (i.e., goals fit with the developmental stage of the program). Fetterman (2001, p. 89) describes empowerment evaluation as using evaluation techniques and findings to "foster improvement and self-determination." Self-determination, a core value inherent in the process, becomes manifest as participants focus on their mission, take stock of what they are doing, and plan for the future (Fetterman, 2001). Participatory evaluation approaches largely place the people who provide and receive services as the participants who make critical decisions about the standards of success, program/organizational practices, lessons learned, and what to share with others (Andrews, 2004). Our approach, like most approaches to participatory evaluation, seeks to minimize the distinctions between the researchers and the participants (Sarri and Sarri, 1992). Participatory approaches recognize shared interests among those doing the work, the people the work is designed to reach, the project funders, and other stakeholders. Brown (1995) points out that the role of the coach in participatory evaluation is one of co-learner, member of the "co-inquiry" team, methodological consultant, collaborator, and equal partner. The coach may bring certain technical expertise and the community/organizational participants may bring unique knowledge of the community or the organization. These resources, however, are not used to exert control over any aspects of the program evaluation process (Nyden and Wiewel, 1992). There is evidence that participatory approaches to evaluation not only build organizational evaluation capacity, but also change organizational attitudes, norms, and practices (Campobasso and Davis, 2001; Hernandez and Visher, 2001). Participatory evaluation builds "evaluative thinking" into the norms of organizations (Sabo, 2004).

Coaching self-evaluation requires a broader range of skills than the "distant observers" of external program evaluation (Brown, 1995). As discussed above, capacity-building consultants must possess the competencies associated with traditional program evaluation. Additionally they need skills in communication, team building, group process, and negotiation (Guba and Lincoln, 1989). Group facilitation skills are essential to effective evaluation through a participatory model (Israel et al., 1994). Further, as cited in Brown (1995, p. 211), evaluators may also need

- pedagogical skills to teach both about evaluation and through evaluation;
- political skills to help assess multiple stakeholders' interests and "incorporate political reality into the evaluation"; and
- the ability both to gain stakeholders' cooperation and trust and to sustain stakeholders' interest and involvement over an extended period of time.

To develop evaluation capacity, the capacity-building consultant must employ the methods associated with empowerment, adult learning, and change as discussed in chapter 2 and must be skilled at facilitating a task-oriented group. The coach also must know how to build accountability into such a task-oriented group. The coach should be able to teach team-building skills, as well as model these skills in interactions with the program team members. In our experience, the style and personality of the coach inevitably influence the content and direction of the capacity-building process (Brown, 1995). The actual practice of building capacity for self-evaluation proceeds as an eclectic, flexible process that is consistent with the intended focus on empowering service providers, administrators, and consumers to monitor their own progress and success. Thus, it is extremely important that the style of the coach be consistent with providing a capacity-building, empowering experience for the participants.

It is equally important for coaches in self-evaluation to find a workable balance between assisting team members as they plan and implement their evaluation and fostering self-reliance in them individually and as a team. The work of evaluation can be difficult and time consuming (Brown, 1995). Defining success in concrete, measurable terms and spending valuable time collecting data are tasks that often do not come naturally to staff trained primarily in human relations and in the helping professions. It is important for a coach to understand the theoretical framework that undergirds capacity building and to translate this theory into systematic steps for building self-efficacy for evaluation within each team. Increased self-efficacy for program evaluation provides the foundation for the attitudinal shift of participants regarding their own ability to carry out evaluation.

Knowledge of Effective Practices Research

Effective coaches need a broad range of knowledge not only in the area of program evaluation but also in diverse areas, such as family service provision. For capacity-building consultants working with programs that serve children and families, early-childhood development, after-school programming, parent education, home visiting, and child maltreatment are just a few of the content areas in which they may need to be knowledgeable. Since no one can be an "expert" in every area of human service, the capacity-building consultant must also have access to the resources needed to advise a program whose theoretical foundations or practical applications lie outside his or her own area of expertise. As discussed in chapter 4, working with a team that has complementary skills and expertise is an excellent way to meet the multiple needs of diverse programs.

In providing technical assistance for program planning, one responsibility of the coach may be to inform the program planning team of interventions shown by research to be effective at ameliorating the identified problem. This information is important for the team to make informed decisions about the program strategies that they will use.

Vignette: Choosing Intervention Strategies in Early Childhood Home Visitation

A new program designed to improve outcomes for teen mothers and their young children received funds from a foundation to hire two home visitors and a program director. During an evaluation planning session with a capacity-building consultant hired by the foundation to develop the program's capacity for self-evaluation, the evaluation team articulated a desired process objective of serving one hundred pregnant and parenting teens each year. Since research in the area of early-childhood home visiting indicates that frequent, personalized home visits are a key ingredient for

(continued)

success of such a program, the capacity-building consultant informed the team that attempting to serve one hundred young clients with only two direct care staff could result in a diluted intervention that probably would not be effective. When the original program planners expressed reluctance to reduce the expected caseload, the capacity-building consultant sent them a summary of the relevant research and asked the team to read it before finalizing their program and evaluation plan. After reading the material, the team decided to reduce the desired caseload to fifty clients, a manageable caseload for two home visitors. Program and evaluation implementation progressed well with this revised program plan. The program was effective in achieving its outcome objectives. When asked to reflect on their original plan for numbers of client served, the evaluation team members, knowing how difficult it had been for their two workers to carry a caseload of twenty-five mothers each, shook their heads at one another and agreed that they had been extremely unrealistic to even imagine they could meet the complex needs of that many clients.

Program staff and administrators typically value information from coaches about research-based intervention strategies and readily incorporate such approaches into their program plans. However, this is not always the case. At times, the evaluation team members have strong convictions about the best way to approach program planning and despite research-based recommendations will insist on other programmatic strategies. Such situations result in a dilemma because using evidence-based strategies is important to program success. However, building evaluation capacity within an agency requires that the staff be empowered by the process and that they develop true ownership for the evaluation. This dilemma can be further complicated if there is an external funder who is aware of the research-based strategies and requests that the program staff change strategies. While such a request is clearly appropriate prior to funding as part of negotiations with those who wrote the proposal, insisting on such change after funding is actually received can be disempowering for the program team and result in resentment and resistance. A capacity-building consultant who is attempting to work within such a climate is challenged to facilitate a way to move forward with program planning. A helpful strategy in these situations is to provide all parties—the program staff, administrators, board members, and funder—with the research recommendations and convene a meeting to further discuss programmatic strategies. In the meeting, the coach will want to discuss potential implications if the team decides not to follow recommended practice, including his or her reluctance to assist the team in conducting an evaluation. As an alternative, the coach may want to negotiate an agreement to examine early evaluation results with the team's preferred plan and reconsider the program plan if progress toward outcomes is not forthcoming. With these conditions met, hopefully the coach and the other members of the team can proceed in both good spirit and good faith. The coach must always be mindful that capacity building is both a learning and an empowering process. Thus whatever actions are taken will ultimately inform the capacity-building efforts.

Another responsibility of the coach is to clarify the importance of evaluating program outcomes. Program staff and administrators may need help in accepting that, though program implementation is a necessary ingredient in success, it is not evidence of program effectiveness. The coach may want to provide some published evaluation results in the area of child and family services to reinforce the message that not all popular program interventions are effective at achieving positive change (e.g., Henggeler and Schoenwald, 1994; Kirby, 2001; Law Enforcement News, 1996). Outcome evaluation, though difficult, is necessary to determine if the resources required to provide the services are justified in terms of significant positive effect on people's lives or the collective life of a neighborhood or community.

Inclusiveness

Inclusiveness is a central value underlying the theoretical frameworks from which self-evaluation grows. Inclusiveness begins with the selection of members of the evaluation team. Establishing a productive evaluation team is essential to a successful self-evaluation effort (Thomas, 2004; Weiss and Jacobs, 1998). Ideally, self-evaluation teams working with the capacity-building consultant will include stakeholders at all levels, such as consumers, direct service providers, administrators, and board members with varying individual perspectives, skills, and concerns. Each team member is included as an "expert" whose views and contributions are equally important as that of the coach, if not more so. Consumers of the services to be provided are essential contributors to the planning and evaluation process; therefore, efforts must be made to obtain and retain their participation in the process, beginning with the planning phase. However, getting genuine stakeholder involvement that includes consumers of services is quite challenging (Mertens, 1999; Thomas, 2004; Weiss and Jacobs, 1988).

Cultural Competence

Another value central to the practice of coaching self-evaluation is that of cultural competence. Building the coach's, as well as the organization's capacity for cultural competence is discussed at length in chapter 3. Becoming a culturally competent organization, one that provides services consistent with the culture of its consumers, is a developmental process. In order to achieve positive outcomes, community programs must work diligently toward cultural competence, realizing that it is a continual process of growth. Evaluation of program implementation and service delivery should involve ongoing assessment of the level of cultural competence achieved by the agency, the program, and the service providers. Moreover, coaches engaged in evaluative efforts should be mindful of the cultural factors relevant to the evaluation process and to the dissemination of the evaluation. A diverse team of engaged stakeholders will increase the likelihood of conducting a culturally competent evaluation. Attention to the multicultural guidelines for research that are relevant to program self-evaluation efforts will greatly enhance program evaluation efforts within diverse cultural contexts (American Psychological Association, 2003; also see discussion in chapter 3 of this book).

BUILDING SELF-EVALUATION CAPACITY: LESSONS LEARNED

The contributors to this volume and their colleagues have provided technical assistance designed to increase agency, organizational, and program capacity for self-evaluation for a number of years. Over these years, we have discovered a number of potentially problematic issues that emerge with surprising consistency across diverse capacity-building efforts. We have also discovered ways to prevent some of these common issues from becoming barriers. This section summarizes the lessons that we have learned in support of effective capacity building.

Funding of Evaluation

In order for organizations to be successful at increasing evaluation capacity, the staff must put a significant amount of time and energy into learning, planning, and conducting program evaluation. If funding is received from an external source, it is often fully earmarked for programming, with no resources dedicated to the staff time needed for evaluation. This lack of designated staff time for evaluation can become a major obstacle to the success of the technical assistance. Often administrators of a program do not realize the time commitment involved in evaluation work and subsequently neither make adjustments in the other responsibilities of those working with the evaluation efforts nor designate any of their own time to perform some of the evaluation tasks. Often the responsibility for the evaluation of a new program is relegated to new staff members hired to implement the program. These staff members can be overwhelmed with the need to learn the policies and procedures at a new job, implement a new program, and lead an evaluation effort. In such situations, we have observed high rates of rapid turnover among new project directors and other staff.

As coaches engage with organizations, it is important to educate the agency or external funder of a new program about the need for broad resources to support the self-evaluation. Attention to issues such as anticipated time, skills, technology, materials, and funds should be discussed in detail with the grantee and the grant maker. Grant makers should be encouraged to help by making resources for evaluation available to grantees and identifying these resources as distinct from the award for program funding. For new programs, funds to support at least a part-time staff member to lead the evaluation effort are extremely valuable. For an existing program, it is helpful to rearrange responsibilities with the added work of evaluation in mind. In all instances, the coach should make sure that everyone at the agency recognizes the difficulty of adding the evaluation tasks to already full work schedules and that the individuals shouldering the responsibility receive the required time and recognition for their efforts and the support and assistance of other staff and administrators. In situations where grantees themselves have chosen to engage in a participatory self-evaluation process, they may be willing to find internal resources to facilitate this capacity-building process.

Emphasizing Outcomes Too Early

An important part of early discussions about the "fit" of capacity-building technical assistance with the stakeholder's needs and expectations is a detailed explanation of the differences in contracting for a traditional, external evaluation and contracting for technical assistance to build the capacity for program self-evaluation. This discussion educates all interested parties about what evaluation products realistically can be expected. It can easily take more than a year for a team to complete a sound program and evaluation plan, begin collecting data, and learn to write reports. Often the outcome evaluation proves most difficult for the team. It is often unrealistic to expect true outcomes or a full-blown sophisticated outcome report at the end of the first year. Unless prepared for this possibility, stakeholders can be disappointed and dissatisfied. If, however, there is agreement that the goal is to facilitate a learning process, expectations can be framed in terms of evidence that learning is occurring at a slow but steady rate. Thus, at the end of one year, stakeholders may realistically expect "progress toward outcomes" rather than the outcomes themselves.

Clarity of Role and Responsibilities

Negotiating contracts before beginning capacity-building work can be invaluable for clarifying the roles and responsibilities of each stakeholder. Carefully identifying the work as either consultation, technical assistance, or outsourcing of services (see chapter 2) will help everyone understand the level of effort expected. In our experience as capacity-building consultants, one of the most frequent areas of misunderstanding we have encountered is lack of clarity concerning who ultimately is responsible for completing the evaluation tasks. Questions are likely to arise regarding who is responsible for developing the evaluation plan, collecting and analyzing the data, and other concrete evidence that progress is being made on the evaluation. At times, there is misunderstanding about who writes the evaluation report for the funder. Does the evaluation team write the required evaluation reports with assistance from the coach, or is the coach responsible, with input from the team? Or does each write a separate report? In order to build capacity within the agency or organization, the responsibility for report writing should be the team's, with guidance from the coach. However, since report writing is a complex skill, reports written by those just beginning to learn how may not appear as polished and complete as those written by an evaluation professional. Unless the time and effort required to learn to write a good evaluation report has been discussed during the early negotiations, dissatisfaction with the end product and with the coach may arise.

Issues of Power, Control, and Leadership

When an organization's capacity building is funded by a source external to the organization, it is important that issues of power, control, and leadership be addressed prior to finalizing the arrangements for technical assistance. Although promoting program self-evaluation has become popular as a way of building accountability into human service programming, this type of evaluation is not a good fit for every funder, every program, or every evaluation professional. For an organization to conduct an evaluation and become empowered to measure its own success, members of the organization must be able to make decisions about the evaluation plan and process. When an external funding source, such as a foundation, state or federal agency, community coalition, or other organization, contracts with a coach or team of coaches to build the capacity of an agency or program for program self-evaluation, power must be shared for the effort to be successful. The funder and coach both must be willing to share control with the program evaluation team and must be flexible in their expectations about the outputs of the capacity-building process.

If the same funder is financing both a program and building evaluation capacity, the financial link between the funder and the coach can make the program staff distrustful of both the coach and the entire capacity-building process. They may view the coach as an agent of the funder whose job it is to spy on them. In our experience, we have found it very helpful to clarify our role as a teacher and mentor who is employed by the funder to support the evaluation process. This clarification is particularly helpful at the beginning of the work with the evaluation team as part of a "getting to know each other" session. Symonette (2004) stresses that "much evaluation is grounded in social relations, and trust is the glue and fuel for cultivating viable and productive social relations" (p. 100). As a consequence, she emphasizes, trust must be promoted systematically and carefully guarded throughout the capacity-building process. Similarly, we find that staff members in nonprofit and other service agencies place great value on time spent forming a relationship with their coach, rather than beginning the process in a more stereotypical efficient, businesslike manner. The coach will do well to devote a portion of each session to fostering a meaningful relationship with program staff.

As they do evaluation work on capacity building, coaches must be sensitive both to the needs of funders for positive results and of program personnel for self-determination. Increasing internal capacity for program self-evaluation depends on the opportunity for the evaluation team to lead the evaluation planning and implementation process, even when team members make mistakes. Equally important is willingness to allow the team to progress at its own pace, even when it fails to meet the funder's expectations for progress. In order to balance the power within the partnership, the funder needs to remain flexible on details of the process such as timeframes, implementation schedule, and the definition of program success. However, flexibility on the part of the funder and the capacity-building consultant must be balanced with a requirement that the program staff and administrators demonstrate reasonable time and effort at learning program self-evaluation and that they show steady progress. Funders are often under pressure from boards or other entities to demonstrate successful use of funds and can be caught in a serious dilemma if the evaluation efforts produce little concrete evidence of success.

Goodness of Fit

After a discussion to clarify the issues of power, control, and leadership, the coach and funder should articulate a decision about the "goodness of fit" between the expectations of the funder and capacity-building technical assistance. If promoting program self-evaluation is consistent with the funder's objectives, the next important task for the capacity-building consultant and representative of the funder is to clarify that the goal is to build the capacity for evaluation within the agency or program, not to accomplish a sophisticated outcome evaluation. In order for the capacity-building process to move at its own pace and direction, the evaluation team must be free to make decisions about the program and evaluation without fear of having funding terminated.

When funders embrace the empowerment of their grantees both in theory and in practice and view the goal of coaching as building evaluation capacity, the result is a partnership in which the capacity-building consultant is seen by the evaluation team as a coach and advocate. According to Fetterman (1994), for empowerment evaluation to be effective and credible, participants must have the latitude to experiment, take risks and responsibility for their actions, and operate in an environment that is conducive to sharing both successes and failures. It is extremely important, however, for the program and agency staff members to be able to be confident that one of the risks of the process does not include loss of funding. Building evaluation capacity requires an atmosphere characterized by support, trust, honesty, and the ability to be self-critical. When the funder, coach, and the evaluation team are in agreement that *building evaluation capacity* is the real goal, this learning environment results.

Shared power, control, and leadership, though necessary, must be delicately balanced with program accountability and the motivation to develop evaluation skills. Sometimes funders are overly flexible and allow program or agency teams to proceed with the coach while paying little attention to indications of progress in building capacity. This lack of attention to the evaluation process can result in disempowerment of the coach, where programs have little interest or motivation to devote the time and effort necessary to increase their evaluation capacity. A danger of this lack of support from the funder for an ongoing evaluation process is that lack of progress becomes an issue as the end of the funding period draws near and can result in conflict and dissatisfaction with the program team and with the capacity-building consultant.

Vignette: Power Triangles

A coach who provides technical assistance to build capacity for program self-evaluation can find himself or herself locked in a dysfunctional triangle with the external funder and program evaluation team. When funder, team, and the capacity-building consultant are focused on their common goal and share equally in power and control, all is balanced and operates smoothly. However, at times the balance of focus and power within the triangle is disrupted. A basic premise of building capacity for evaluation is that the grantee will choose intended results and strategies to achieve the results. When this is the common goal of all parties, the grantee feels supported and exerts energy to do well. When the funder or coach have different ideas and try to exert influence to change the grantee's intended results or strategies, the grantee is likely to resist and progress slows.

For example, a youth development program near a high-risk neighborhood decided to make office-based family counseling available. The funder and capacity-building consultant knew that effective practices research indicated that the no-show rate for office-based services would be high and that home-based outreach was indicated for communities like the one served by this program. They agreed with the intended outcome of the grantee, which was to reduce parent-child conflicts, but they disagreed with the strategy. The grantee staff members were not comfortable providing home-based services and felt that the funder was pushing them around. The staff delayed doing anything to serve the families. The capacity-building consultant agreed with the best practices approach and tried to help the grantee learn about home-based services. Although staff members were polite and attended training sessions, they continued to provide office-based services and became resistant to the evaluation technical assistance. Little progress was made in capacity building or in the evaluation itself.

BUILDING CAPACITY FOR SELF EVALUATION: MEASURING SUCCESS

What does a coach actually *do* to help a program build its capacity to measure its own success? Early in our capacity-building work, we asked ourselves this question. We understood our multiple roles as coaches and the theories underlying program self-evaluation. We believed in participation, inclusiveness, and being culturally competent. Although there are handbooks and manuals for individuals or groups who want to learn evaluation skills (Fitz-Gibbon and Morris, 1987; Fitzpatrick, Sanders, and Worthen, 2003; Wholey, Hatry, and Newcomer, 1994), we found little in the way of step-by-step, specific guidance for *coaches* who do work building evaluation capacity.

The methods described here are those we have found through practice to be effective in building capacity for self-evaluation. Our approach to building this capacity combines an initial training session on the core concepts and practices of program evaluation followed by a period of ongoing technical assistance. Both the training and technical assistance, consistent with a capacity-building approach, focus on the strengths of the participants and are designed to increase their self-confidence as program evaluators and to build their skills to conduct their own evaluation. Efforts focus on empowering the staff of the agency or organization to take charge of assessing their own program success. The steps of this process are presented below (Andrews et al., 2005; Flerx, 1999). The detailed discussion that follows will be especially useful for readers who have limited experience offering this type of technical assistance or coaching.

STEPS IN BUILDING CAPACITY FOR SELF-EVALUATION

1. Assessment of readiness
2. Initial training
   - Preparation for initial training
   - Clarification of purpose of capacity-building technical assistance
   - Evaluation basics
   - Work session for evaluation team with coach on logic model
3. On-site technical assistance
   - Continued work sessions with coach to complete logic model
   - Coaching to develop evaluation plan
   - Support for data collection and analysis
   - Facilitate interpretation of data and use for program improvement

- Support for report writing
- Setting up a management information system
4. Distance technical assistance and coaching
   - Conducted by e-mail, phone, fax
   - Establish accountability of evaluation team
   - Support for team between on-site sessions
5. Interagency meetings on periodic basis
   - Establish peer support
   - Group problem solving regarding obstacles
   - Share successes
   - Share lessons learned

Assessing Readiness for Self-Evaluation

The ultimate success of the capacity-building effort depends on agency and program readiness. Organizational change theory (see discussion in chapter 2 of this volume) is the organizing framework for assessing the needed conditions for motivation or readiness to engage in an activity such as self-evaluation. When the technical assistance provided by the coach is funded by a source external to the organization, the tenets of change theory are equally important in assessing the necessary conditions for funder readiness. Thus, one of the initial tasks of a coach is to assess the readiness of both funder and program/agency for the capacity-building work in order to determine if program self-evaluation "fits" with the needs and expectations of everyone involved. This assessment begins with conversations with key stakeholders prior to contract negotiations and continues as an ongoing part of these. As a case study in chapter 2 illustrates (see "Vignette: Sometimes Capacity Isn't Built: An Example Highlighting the Importance of Assessing Readiness and Maintaining Contractual Roles"), assessing readiness is an essential component in capacity building. We have used the following checklist for assessing a program's readiness for evaluation capacity building.

ASSESSMENT OF READINESS CHECKLIST

√ Stakeholders understand the difference between the products of capacity-building technical assistance and an external program evaluation

√ Staff members of program/agency understand and accept the expectation that they will learn to evaluate their program and will produce evaluation reports

√ Staff of agency/program is large enough to provide an evaluation team to share responsibility for program evaluation

√ Program has infrastructure to support on-site and distance technical assistance sessions

√ Buy-in for building the capacity for evaluation is evident at both administrative and direct service levels

Clarification of Stakeholders' Expectations for Program and Agency Staff

While clarification of expectations is fundamental to all technical assistance, it is even more important when a self-evaluation effort is funded by an external entity. In such instances, it is important that the agency and program staff be informed early of the funder's expectation that they will learn to conduct self-evaluation. If the agency itself is contracting with a coach, the entire staff should be informed and those who will be expected to learn and perform self-evaluation should be identified. Everyone who is to be involved in the evaluation should understand that participation in the initial training and the ongoing coaching is a requirement of the agency, the funder, or whatever entity has made the decision. The ideal situation, one that can only sometimes be arranged, is one in which the staff members themselves have chosen to participate in learning and conducting self-evaluation rather than agreeing to learn self-evaluation in fulfillment of an externally imposed requirement.

Stakeholders' Understanding of Products of Building Evaluation Capacity

The products of building evaluation capacity will differ from those of an external evaluation. Learning to produce logic models (strategies for linking program theory to program activities and outcomes), evaluation plans, and evaluation reports takes time. As noted earlier, the stakeholders must accept that the learning process will be slow and that the products of the evaluation team may be much less sophisticated than those of a consultant hired to conduct an external evaluation as an out-sourced service. Funders should be prepared to educate their boards about these differences at the beginning of the capacity-building process so that dissatisfaction with the capacity-building consultant and program staff is avoided. All stakeholders should agree to measure early success by evidence of progress being made by the evaluation team.

An Evaluation Team

When discussing the requirements of self-evaluation, it is important to stress that each program will need an evaluation team to participate in the training and to plan and implement the evaluation. As discussed earlier, this team should be diverse and include a representative of key stakeholders, including at least one agency or program administrator, one direct service provider, a consumer, and a board member of the agency. The responsibility for the evaluation should rest on the team, not on any one individual. If the agency is unable or unwilling to form a team of several people who are responsible for planning and implementing the evaluation, serious consideration should be given to whether it might be a better choice for the organization or program to retain an outside evaluator to conduct the evaluation. An external evaluation may be more appropriate and more feasible in the case of a small program that is not nested within a larger agency or organization or is in an agency in which administrators of the agency are not willing to assume a share of the evaluation work. The small size of the direct service staff typically working in such a program, particularly when the program is new, makes it almost impossible to both implement a program and conduct a self-evaluation.

After an evaluation team is selected, the team should ask one person to serve as the contact for the evaluation coach. Team members should expect to meet frequently. Weekly meetings probably will be necessary during the planning and start-up phases of the effort. The frequency of these meetings, however, will vary during the life of the capacity-building effort.

Infrastructure, "Buy-In," and Time for Planning

The capacity of an organization to learn program self-evaluation is enhanced by supportive infrastructure. Having access to a computer with Internet and e-mail capabilities and to fax and copy machines is almost as important for success as is having sufficient person power to carry out the work of evaluation. Although teams with little supportive infrastructure certainly can be successful when sufficiently motivated, the capacity-building consultant and funder should assess this factor as part of determining readiness.

As emphasized previously, staff "buy-in," or the degree to which staff members are internally motivated to learn program self-evaluation, is extremely important for success in capacity building. However, accurately assessing staff buy-in is often difficult. Sometimes meeting with staff members who will be on the evaluation team without the administrators present can be useful for assessing this aspect of readiness. However, in cases where participation is required by the external funder, it is unlikely that the coach will be able to get a true sense of buy-in until the technical assistance is underway.

The coach's support is critical during the initial period of the planning and implementation process. The staff will be attempting to perform the evaluation tasks as well as either implement a new program or continue to provide services of an existing program. When the coaching is with a new program, allowing a minimum of three months for program and evaluation planning prior to beginning service delivery is recommended. Programs that begin service delivery immediately often go forward with a program plan that is vague or in which the target population, goals, and objectives of the program are not well defined. Problems can be prevented when team members work with the coach for a few months to refine the program plan using the logic model and to plan the evaluation. For example, new programs that begin service delivery prior to completing their evaluation plan frequently realize, when the first evaluation report is due, that they neglected to collect baseline data on their pre- and postintervention measures.

Such a planning period also helps prevent program staff and administrators from feeling overwhelmed by the work involved in learning and planning their own program evaluation. Attempting to begin new service delivery and learn evaluation at the same time can result in staff burnout and turnover. Even when a program has been providing services for some time before beginning the self-evaluation technical assistance, staff may feel stretched by the need to change or refine program strategies as a result of the work on the logic model. Existing programs typically do not collect the kind of data needed for an adequate process evaluation and often have collected no outcome data prior to beginning the technical assistance. Staff of these programs may also feel overwhelmed at the beginning of the self-evaluation process.

Initial Training

If assessment indicates that an organization is ready to build evaluation capacity, one effective way to begin the process is to conduct an initial training session for the evaluation team on the fundamentals of evaluation. An important goal of such training is to help participants understand the differences between program implementation and program success. Typically, four to five hours should be allotted for the initial training. This is a long time for people to stay involved in a didactic session, so attention to adult learning strategies is recommended. Similarly, the training room should be set up to encourage active rather than passive learning. For example, arranging the seats in a semicircle or in a circle around a table usually leads to more interaction than when participants are sitting in rows of desks or chairs. The evaluation materials should be designed to foster participation and interaction. The following sections of this chapter present an overview of the content of initial training that we have provided to family and child–serving agencies and organizations. This overview may be used as a guide with the materials presented in the inserts or with similar materials selected by the reader.

Beginning the Initial Training

Consistent with an adult learning approach, an initial training session in an effort to build self-evaluation capacity begins with setting the stage for active learning. We begin with a series of questions that stimulate discussion of the definition, purpose, and relevance of program evaluation (Flerx, 1999). Further questions explore participants' feelings related to evaluation. For example, the members of the evaluation team are asked to write their own answers to questions such as "what is evaluation?" and "why do evaluation?" and then to brainstorm answers with the whole group to elicit participation. Often team members may seem resistant or anxious because they do not feel competent at evaluation or may fear that if the evaluation has negative results, the programs' funding or their own jobs may be jeopardized. Reinforcing the group's responses by displaying slides or overheads that contain similar "answers" is important for increasing the participants' comfort with evaluation and for increasing confidence in their ability to perform program evaluation, thus facilitating the process of capacity building. The following is a list of questions typically used in initial training.

WHAT IS A PROGRAM?

A program is . . .

- any series of activities
- supported by resources
- intended to achieve specific outcomes

What is program evaluation?

- a process by which staff/stakeholders are able to determine progress toward goals

- an assessment of the extent to which an intervention or service achieves its objectives
- a determination of congruence between the performance of a program and its objectives

Why perform program evaluation?

- to make decisions about whether to continue or modify an intervention or service
- to determine strengths/barriers related to success
- to determine additional resource needs
- to determine if the program works
- to determine cost/effectiveness

What are five things about evaluation that make people nervous?

- don't know how
- don't have time
- not good at statistics
- not enough money
- too much paperwork
- fear that the evaluation may show that the program isn't working

Why do evaluation?

- more likely to achieve its goals if they are defined and measured
- evaluation provides a tool for obtaining and maintaining funding and support
- evaluation helps the organization know if its activities are reaching the intended groups
- evaluation identifies the effective elements of the project and the areas that need improvement
- evaluation documents organizational efforts and allows the organization to inform itself and others about what did and did not work
- evaluation will help the organization figure out if its program is working as intended

(*Source*: Flerx, 1999)

Evaluation Basics

Within the initial training, it is important to present information on the basics of evaluation; core concepts such as "goals," "objectives," and "strategies" should be defined. The important role of the logic model for program and evaluation planning should be explained.

Since the terminology used by different experts to label various evaluation-related concepts varies, participants are often confused about the concepts and the terms. The coach should be careful to explain each concept clearly, provide all the terms commonly used for the concept, and then present the set of terms that he or she prefers to use. If the coach is training only one team (often multiple teams, funded within a common initiative are trained together), the coach may encourage group members to decide which terminology they wish to use.

BASIC EVALUATION CONCEPTS TO TEACH

- Program planning and evaluation should occur simultaneously
- A clearly articulated program plan is the first step for both program development and evaluation planning
- The broad goals of the program must be broken down into objectives that are specific, observable, and measurable
- The target population must be well-defined
- There must be a theoretical link between the goals and objectives, the program activities (strategies/interventions), and the desired outcomes
- Program evaluation includes an assessment of the program's success in implementation (process evaluation), as well as in achieving the desired outcomes (outcome evaluation)
- A successful program achieves outcomes that match the outcome objectives set during the planning phase

(*Source*: Flerx, 1999)

COMMON EVALUATION TERMS TO TEACH

Goal: Broad, general statement concerning what a program intends to accomplish.

Objective: Specific, measurable statement describing what program intends to accomplish.

Target group/population: Person, organization, community, or other clearly identified group that the program intends to affect.

Inputs: Resources needed to achieve program objectives. Inputs support activities.

Program activities: Also known as "strategies" or "interventions." Activities are what a program does or the services it provides. Activities result in outputs.

Outputs: Products of the program's activities. Outputs contribute to success in achieving outcome objectives.

Outcomes: The changes that the program seeks to achieve. The change can be in an individual, in a population or community, or in an organization/system. Programs usually achieve both short-term (6–18 months) and long-term outcomes.

Logic model: a diagram that shows the links between the problem or need that the program addresses, the program components, and the proposed outcomes (outcome objectives) of the program.

(*Source*: Flerx, 1999)

Teamwork During the Initial Training

Each program should require its entire evaluation team to participate in the initial training session. As discussed in the previous section on readiness, team members should know prior to the initial training that they are expected to participate in both the initial training and the ongoing technical assistance and that they will be responsible for the evaluation. Following the training in core evaluation terms and concepts, team members work together to begin developing a logic model for their program. The logic model helps service providers verify that their program plan is sound by separating the plan into component parts. Each part is reviewed for clarity, and then the whole plan is examined to make sure there is a good fit between the expressed goals, selected strategies, and the desired outcomes. A specific, theory-based program plan is a prerequisite to developing a good evaluation plan. Even if the program plan was developed with great care prior to beginning the process of building evaluation capacity, it will typically need to be reexamined and refined through the logic model process.

The logic model is also a helpful tool for building group consensus on the specifics of a program under development. There is often some degree of ambiguity in a program plan even after it is funded and implemented, and different staff may have different perceptions of the strategies that should be used to produce the desired changes. In addition, the desired outcomes are often stated in general terms that cannot be articulated in measurable objectives. Coming to consensus on the specifics of the program by developing a logic model will strengthen the initial program plan and ensure that everyone has a similar understanding of the program. A number of different logic model formats have been published in program evaluation manuals during the past few years (Fetterman, 2003; United Way of America, 1996). Regardless of which format is used, it is important for the coach to point out to the team on numerous occasions that the value of the logic model lies not in the form itself but in the process by which the team develops the specifics of the program's theoretical framework. Evaluation team members often view the form on which their logic model is recorded as merely a bit of necessary paperwork to be filed away when completed. It is helpful to ask the team to review the model at each consultation and make adjustments or changes as needed. We have found the set of worksheets reproduced in figure 6.1 useful in helping evaluation teams develop a meaningful logic model for their program.

Teamwork on the logic model during the initial training is an excellent way for the team to apply the information that was presented in the basic evaluation training. It also sets the scene for team members' subsequent work together and for the evaluation coaching sessions that will follow the training. Participants often report that working on the logic model is the most valuable part of the training, so one should allow at least several hours for the team to work together. The success of this initial working session depends on having a skilled coach guiding the process. If multiple evaluation teams are trained together, it is important that one or more additional capacity-building consultants assist with this part of the training so that each team has a coach available to facilitate their work.

As discussed previously, in developing a new program, program success is linked to theory-based and research-based interventions; therefore, the team should be encouraged to choose research-based interventions for the specified target population. For example, a teen pregnancy prevention program whose staff members are planning to provide a combination of abstinence and contraception education might be encouraged to broaden the scope of their strategies and include evidence-based interventions, such as a program of activities systematically planned to present teens with realistic alternatives for their futures (Kirby, 1997; Kirby, Barth, Leland, and Fetro, 1991; Lagana and Hayes, 1993; Miller and Card, 1992).

ON-SITE TECHNICAL ASSISTANCE

As soon after the initial training as possible, it is good practice to schedule an on-site technical assistance session with the team. This supports the team's

Following on pages 162–165

FIGURE 6.1 Worksheets for Development of Logic Model

Worksheet #1
Need or Condition

What is the need or condition that your agency or group wants to address?

_____
_____
_____
_____
_____
_____
_____
_____
_____
_____

Worksheet #2
Goals of Program

What change does your program hope to accomplish in response to this need?

_____
_____
_____
_____
_____
_____
_____
_____
_____

Worksheet #3
Identifying Target Group

What specific group of residents does your program hope to assist? (i.e., age, gender location of residence, socio-economic group)

_____

_____

_____

_____

_____

_____

_____

Worksheet #4
Identifying Necessary Inputs

What resources are needed to make the program possible?

From your agency

_____

From community/consumers

_____

From volunteers

_____

From partners/collaborators

_____

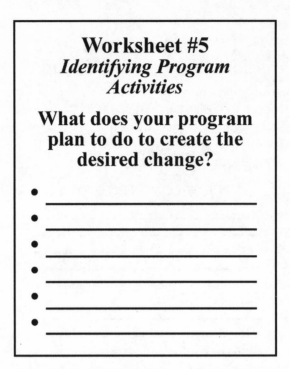

Worksheet #5
Identifying Program Activities

What does your program plan to do to create the desired change?

- _____
- _____
- _____
- _____
- _____
- _____

Worksheet #6
Identifying Target Group

What products will result from the program activities?

_____
_____
_____
_____
_____
_____
_____
_____
_____

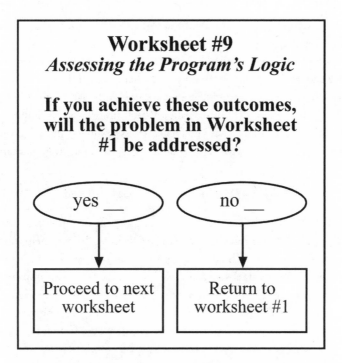

Worksheet #9
Assessing the Program's Logic

If you achieve these outcomes, will the problem in Worksheet #1 be addressed?

yes __   no __

| Proceed to next worksheet | Return to worksheet #1 |

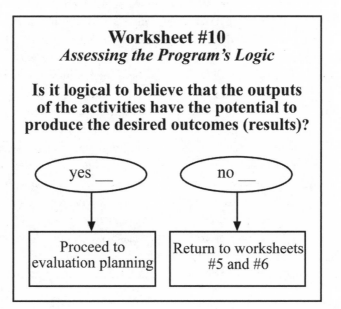

Worksheet #10
Assessing the Program's Logic

Is it logical to believe that the outputs of the activities have the potential to produce the desired outcomes (results)?

yes __   no __

| Proceed to evaluation planning | Return to worksheets #5 and #6 |

efforts to develop a logic model without loss of momentum. Completing the logic model can easily take several sessions with the coach.

Following completion of the logic model, the focus of the ongoing technical assistance should turn to (1) developing an evaluation plan that reflects the logic model; (2) documenting a specific data-collection and analysis plan; (3) writing an evaluation report; and (4) using data for continuous program improvement. Attention to cultural competence and inclusiveness should be infused throughout these initial efforts as well as all aspects of program and evaluation planning.

Coaching Development of an Evaluation Plan

After an evaluation team has completed the program planning and has finalized a logic model, the team will need intensive coaching to help develop a detailed evaluation plan. The purpose of this plan is to set specific criteria for success, determine the data source for each specific criterion or objective, and decide how the data will be analyzed and used. As with the logic model, there are a number of different ways that an evaluation plan can be written. The worksheets in figure 6.2 use a format that has proven effective for a number of the evaluation teams with whom we have consulted.

Although most programs are accustomed to doing process evaluation, which involves recording data and reporting on variables like participation rates and services delivered, staff members are sometimes not familiar with outcome evaluation.[2] Even though the initial training is designed to help participants understand the difference between program implementation and program success, it is a good idea to reiterate this information during the on-site technical assistance. Outcomes can be at an individual, family, agency, or community level. Many programs that focus on services to a limited number of individuals make the mistake of setting outcome objectives based on changing community-level statistical indicators. In such cases, the coach will need to help the team set realistic outcome objectives. For example, in a teen pregnancy prevention program that will serve approximately 140 teens each year, it would not be realistic to set "reduce pregnancy rate in *Any County* by 15 percent" as an outcome objective. Rather than a community-level outcome objective, an objective for a small pregnancy prevention program should be based on the program participants and their incidence of pregnancy. An

---

2. Readers who are unfamiliar with the definitions of process and outcome evaluation are referred to the United Way of America's excellent manual, *Measuring Program Outcomes: A Practical Approach* (1996).

EVALUATION PLAN WORKSHEET 1: INPUTS

Organization and Program: _____   Date: _____

Inputs	Indicators	Data Source	Data Analysis & Use

FIGURE 6.2: Evaluation Plan Worksheets (*continued on pages 168–169*)

EVALUATION PLAN WORKSHEET 2: OUTPUTS

Organization and Program: _____ Date: _____

Inputs	Indicators	Data Source	Data Analysis & Use

EVALUATION PLAN WORKSHEET 3: OUTCOMES

Organization and Program: _____   Date: _____

Inputs	Indicators	Data Source	Data Analysis & Use

attainable outcome objective based on the participating population might be, for example, "No more than 5 percent of teens who participate in the program for the entire year will become pregnant during the year or for one year after completing the program."

Data Sources and Data-Collection Methods

Specifying the sources from which process and outcome assessment data will be gathered helps the team begin to think of the evaluation in a more concrete way. This process seems to move the team from thinking of evaluation as an abstract, rather nebulous process, to viewing the evaluation in the context of their daily activities. Typical data sources for process evaluation are program records and logs such as volunteer rosters and time sheets, schedules of groups and workshops, minutes of meetings, client files and records, attendance sheets for activities, and service provider daily logs or appointment sheets. Program consumers, staff members, community leaders, and others have important data for process evaluation. Such data may be most easily accessed through surveys or interviews. In documenting data sources on the evaluation plan, the staff of the program will probably realize that some process data of the program are not being recorded in a systematic way. The task of the coach is often to assist the staff as they develop and begin using a form or other source for each data item or variable.

Often school records related to attendance, behavioral difficulties, grades, and other school data sources are chosen by evaluation teams of youth-serving programs. Due to privacy rights and school policies and practices, these data are often difficult to obtain from schools. Even when obtained, inconsistencies in format may make the information unusable. If school data are important to assessing program implementation and program outcomes, then school involvement is also important to overall program success. Thus, the coach should encourage the team to actively recruit the school as a partner in the project. As a partner, the school representative is likely to be more vested in program outcomes and may be able to facilitate obtaining the needed data.

Another important role of the coach is to help the evaluation team decide what data are relevant and necessary to collect. Sometimes when teams get excited about evaluation, they want to collect data that are interesting but not central to the program or the evaluation plan. At least at the beginning of the program's efforts at self-evaluation, it is wise to collect only data that are needed to assess successful implementation of the program and positive outcomes.

Whenever possible, data sources for individual outcome objectives should be standardized instruments or measures that have been developed and validated by research. More confidence is warranted in evaluation results based on data collected by standardized measures than can be placed in results of measures developed by the program itself. While standardized measures are often copyrighted, there are numerous assessment instruments, questionnaires, observational tools, and rating scales available in the public domain or for very little cost (Caldwell and Bradley, 1984; Impara and Plake, 1998; Jones, 1996; Linney and Wandersman, 1991; Rosenberg, 1965).

Helping the evaluation team decide how to measure program outcomes is often one of the most difficult tasks of the coach, but it is essential to measuring program success. The instruments selected for documenting outcomes must actually measure what the evaluation team intends to measure. As noted in chapter 3, consultants and program staff consistently encounter challenges as they seek outcome measures that are culturally relevant. Many instruments have not been normed or tested with diverse populations or do not include relevant items. Thus, locating the right assessment tool can be a difficult task. Researching the academic literature, searching evaluation Web sites, and consulting with assessment experts are all strategies for locating the best measures to document program outcomes. Sometimes a thorough search for an existing instrument fails to identify any suitable measure or at least one that is reasonable to time limits, budgets, and staff resources to make it feasible for program use. At such times, the coach will need to assist the program staff in developing an original measure.

Data can also be collected about program outcomes through qualitative methods, such as interviews and focus groups, participant observation, and case studies. Seeking multiple perspectives or points of view regarding program outcomes and using multiple methods for collecting evaluation information ground the evaluation in the experience of program participants, staff, funders, and others (Drisko, 1997; Glesne, 1999; Hess, McGowan, and Botsko, 2003; Spradley, 1980; Stake, 1995). The use of multiple methods and accessing multiple perspectives provides an inclusive picture of program process and outcomes, enhances stakeholders' confidence regarding the evaluation findings, and provides contextual, process, and other information that is extremely useful in interpreting evaluation findings. The use of multiple methods for collecting data and a variety of data sources has been termed triangulation (Denzin, 1978; Stake, 1995; Thomas, 2004).

The use of open-ended survey questions and of in-depth interviews or focus groups with program participants, staff, community professionals, and other relevant constituencies provides perspectives and experiences that cannot easily be captured through quantitative methods (Denzin and Lincoln, 1994; Glesne, 1999; Morgan, 1993; SenGupta, Hopson, and Thompson-Robinson, 2004). Glesne (1999) notes that the special strength of interviewing is the opportunity "to learn about what you cannot see and to explore alternative explanations of what you do see" (p. 69). Interviews can be designed so that all respondents are asked the same questions or designed as open-ended in order to capture respondents' unique experiences. Glesne (1999), Fetterman (1989), Patton (1990), and many others provide useful guidance in developing and carrying out interviews.

Focus groups, sometimes referred to as group interviews, yield similar benefits and are sometimes more cost and time efficient than conducting a number of individual interviews. It is important to note, however, that depending upon the topic, those providing the information may be more or less comfortable being a part of a group interview as compared to being interviewed individually. Thus, the nature of the information sought, respondents' comfort, and the time available for data collection should all be major determinants in deciding whether to conduct group or individual interviews or to conduct a combination of both. Morgan (1993) examines basic principles regarding focus groups, as well as provides practical discussions on designing and conducting focus groups and analyzing data collected through this method.

Vignette: Interviews with Program Consumers

Over a three-year period, contributors to this volume provided technical assistance related to the development and evaluation of twelve community partnerships formed to meet the needs of children and families (Floyd et al., 2003). The foundation that funded the initiative provided coaching to the partnerships as one aspect of their assistance. Near the conclusion of the funding period, telephone interviews were conducted with twenty-two key participants associated with the partnerships served by the initiative (Hess and Flerx, 2003). An interview guide was developed collaboratively to provide consistent questions across all interviews, which ranged from fifteen minutes to an hour in length. When all interviews were completed, two consultants independently analyzed all interview responses, compared their analyses, and identified emerging categories and themes. These were organized into two broad categories: (1) ways in which the consultation benefited the partnerships and their programs,

(*continued*)

and (2) difficulties related to the consultation. Benefits identified by consumers of the coaches' services included such categories as identifying tasks and staying focused throughout the multiyear process; "coaching us through"—giving feedback, encouragement, support, and ideas; learning skills in using a logic model for program and evaluation planning; and helping the partnership members "think outside the box." Responding consumers included two types of difficulties: (1) difficulties related to the overall coaching model, particularly the timing of the introduction of the coach's services to the partnership, and (2) individual coaching style. Difficulties related to the model included that coaches should be available earlier in the process, (e.g., before funding); grantees should be provided greater and earlier clarity about the services that could be provided by the coach; and more time should be provided in the beginning of the process to get to know the coach. Findings were presented in a manner that did not identify interview consumer respondents or the partnerships with which they were associated. The findings were used as the basis for recommendations about the technical assistance process in future projects. The recommendations were made to the organization and capacity-building consultants providing the coaching as well as to the foundation funding the initiative.

Participant observation is another approach to collecting qualitative information concerning the actual experiences of program staff and participants (Spradley, 1980). Drisko (1997) emphasizes that participant observation is not only an appropriate method for collecting information but also allows "a check of how the [interview and agency record] texts correspond to enacted programs, staff member behaviors, and client reactions" (p. 190).

The systematic development of one or more case studies can be extremely effective in "telling the story" of the program overall or of several program participants. Stake (1995) notes that "A case study is expected to catch the complexity of a single case. . . . We study a case when it itself is of very special interest. . . . Each one [case] is similar to other persons and programs in many ways and unique in many ways. We are interested in them for both their uniqueness and commonality. We seek to understand them" (pp. xi, 1). Program evaluations may be designed as a case study of the entire program (see, for example, Hess et al., 2003) or may include case studies as examples of findings reported (see, for example, Floyd et al., 2003).

Data Collection and Analysis

Coaches can promote accountability for data collection and analysis and report writing by assisting team members in assigning responsibility for specific tasks (e.g., documenting the name of the staff member responsible for each task and the dates for completion) on a formal written plan for data collection and analysis. Figure 6.3 shows a sample form that we created to help our evaluation teams plan their data collection and analysis.

Although outcome data probably will not be available until at least the end of the first year, developing an accountability plan at the beginning of the program implementation will help avoid common problems such as failure to collect preintervention or other baseline data. Coaching the team in completing this form, or a similar one, shortly after the evaluation plan has been completed is recommended. Further, advising the team to use the dates of any internal or external reports as guides for determining the exact deadline for data collection to be done is an excellent strategy for establishing timelines. It is important to help the team set realistic time frames and allow ample time to meet report deadlines. Extra time will need to be built into the schedule if the team wants the coach to review the reports before they are finalized.

Coaching Program Staff in Data Analysis

This component of the data collection and analysis plan designates the methods that will be used to examine or analyze the data collected on the inputs, outputs, and outcomes. Process data collected through quantitative approaches are usually analyzed by simple frequency counts, percentages, and rates. For instance, the process data related to number, frequency, and duration of tutoring in an after-school program could be analyzed by such methods as, "compute the number of children who receive weekly tutoring sessions that last at least forty-five minutes." Other methods of analyzing process data are "calculate percentages," "calculate completion rates," "calculate the mean (average) amount of time volunteered," and other ways of compiling descriptive statistics.

Process data collected through qualitative methods, such as through interviews, participant observation, and case study methods, are usually analyzed by identifying categories, themes, patterns, and issues in the transcriptions of interviews, responses to open-ended survey questions, or thorough notes taken during interviews and participant observations (Fetterman, 1989; Glesne, 1999; Krippendorff, 1980; Morgan, 1993; Patton, 1990; Spradley, 1980; Stake, 1995). As long as individuals' confidentiality and anonymity are protected, verbatim quotations may be used effectively as one component of

DATA COLLECTION AND ANALYSIS PLAN

#	Output/Outcome Objective	Source	Dates Due	Staff Responsible	Date Completed
1					
2					
3					
4					
5					
6					

FIGURE 6.3: Data Collection and Analysis Plan Form

reported findings. Selected quotations can illustrate the categories, themes, and patterns found through data analysis.

Analysis of outcome data collected through quantitative methods can be more sophisticated. One common method used by programs that focus on services to individuals to analyze pre- and postintervention change is to calculate the difference in a score on the baseline administration of a measure and a postintervention administration of the same measure (commonly referred to as a "pre/post-test"). More sophisticated designs and measures may be used for individual-level data, but it is not the norm for initial efforts at program evaluation (Wholey, Hatry, and Newcomer, 1994).

Sometimes community-level statistics on outcomes, such as pregnancy rates, high school dropout rates, and unemployment rates, are collected on a yearly or other regular basis and compared over time. This type of analysis is sometimes suitable to determine the long-term success of a program that is large enough to permeate a particular community. Like other nonexperimental designs, when this data analysis shows positive change over time on the outcomes, success cannot be attributed conclusively to the program. However, such findings can be interpreted as an indication of success, particularly if similar analysis is done on a similar community in which the program does not operate.

Coaching Teams in Data Interpretation and Use

The goal of coaching data interpretation and use is to help the evaluation team understand all the beneficial ways they can use results of the program evaluation. Three important uses of the data from any program evaluation are (1) continuous program improvement, (2) reporting to a funding source, and (3) applying for funding. A coach should help program staff not only to accept responsibility for carrying out their evaluation but also to experience the evaluation process as one that has direct benefits for them and their program. Since evaluation does require considerable work, staff must feel that it is helpful and necessary to ensure program quality before they will begin to "own" the process and use the data for ongoing program improvement.

Writing Program Evaluation Reports

Most agency and program administrators and staff members of children and family service organizations are accustomed to writing periodic reports to a funder, a board, or other stakeholder. Often these reports are primarily narrative, discussing implementation of the program, presenting anecdotal "successes," "challenges," and future directions. Data related to service provision, such as number of children seen, number of home visits, and number of parents attending particular events are often included, as well as examples of individual children or families who have profited from the program. The capacity-building consultant will usually need to coach the team in a systematic way to include quantitative and qualitative data in their report.

The contributors to this volume have developed a practice technique called "Start at the End" (Andrews, 2004) that "involves stakeholders, as a group, framing relatively detailed reports and other products before the evaluation process is conducted" (p. 275). Andrews reports that

> these 'boilerplate' products, called report templates, become the guides for decisions as the planning, implementation, and evaluation of the program proceeds. The templates . . . are specifically designed by the stakeholders who plan to use the evaluation results and written with interpretative evaluation comments in mind. In advance of the program delivery and evaluation, stakeholders are encouraged to anticipate the story they hope to tell about the program and begin to write it.
>
> (p. 275)

A sample generic outline or template for final evaluation reports is depicted in the appendix. This template can be used by the coach with stakeholders to develop the various components of a draft report or draft reports for different audiences. Through the process of using the template to develop a draft report, stakeholders and the evaluation team are able to determine the feasibility of producing the desired information with the evaluation plan they have developed and to make necessary adjustments prior to implementing the plan. Further, by "Starting at the End" stakeholders also clarify standards for the evaluative judgments that must be made (p. 285).

Andrews (2002, p. 277) stresses the following reasons for early product planning:

1. Participants in CBOs [community-based organizations] who are learning participative or empowerment evaluation need concrete images of what the process will produce (otherwise they question the benefit of the evaluation process relative to its costs);
2. Early consensus among multiple stakeholders about the specific format and content of evaluation products builds teamwork and reduces tension or conflict; and

3. Clear expectations regarding products facilitate smoother decision making as the evaluation planning and process evolves; for example, selection of measures is easier when the intended statements about program results are clearly known.

Another tool that we have found helpful for many programs is a form similar to the evaluation plan but with sections for "level of attainment" for each intended output and outcome. This form also provides a space for comments so that the report writer can provide information on any barriers, unusual successes, or changes related to the evaluation results. A copy of this form, "Level of Attainment Form," appears in figure 6.4.

Setting Up a Management Information System (MIS)

It is important for the program to develop an information management system to support evaluation. Whether this system is on paper or computerized will depend on the size, personnel, and resources of each program.

A good paper system for data collection is prerequisite to a computerized system. It is advisable to wait for at least six months or even a year of service delivery and data collection before designing a computerized system for data management. A review of the paper system that was set up as part of the evaluation plan is advisable after the first major report written by the program. A central focus of this assessment should be the relative ease or difficulty with which the staff member who actually wrote the report was able to obtain the needed data to report on the attainment of the program objectives. Timelines and deadlines for compiling data may need to be renegotiated at this point.

It is important that program staff know that an information system cannot solve any existing program problems or answer any questions unless the relevant data are reliably entered. Rather, an information system is a method for storing data that will be used to generate reports. Gaps in service delivery or problems in program administration are often revealed by the process of setting up a MIS, and this identification can be an important first step to program improvement.

DISTANCE TECHNICAL ASSISTANCE AND COACHING

Coaching via telephone conference calls, video conferencing, e-mail, and fax is helpful to keep the team progressing between on-site sessions. Use of such distance technical assistance also helps to establish accountability for completing evaluation tasks in a timely manner. If the team assigns an individual to be

REPORT ON LEVEL OF ATTAINMENT: INPUTS

Organization and Program: _____   Date: _____

Input Indicators/Targets	Level of Attainment	Comments

FIGURE 6.4: Level of Attainment Forms (*pages 179–181*)

REPORT ON LEVEL OF ATTAINMENT: OUTPUTS

Organization and Program: _____ Date: _____

Input Indicators/Targets	Level of Attainment	Comments

REPORT ON LEVEL OF ATTAINMENT: OUTCOMES

Organization and Program: _____   Date: _____

Input Indicators/Targets	Level of Attainment	Comments

responsible for each evaluation task and sets a deadline for completion and the coach follows up at the established time, team members stay focused on the capacity-building process even when a visit from the coach is not imminent. It is important for the coach to support the meeting of deadlines by providing feedback to the team at the established time. Further, it is important that the coach meet his or her assigned tasks as scheduled. Modeling accountability in this way usually results in other team members following suit.

Distance technical assistance, particularly by phone, is also an important means of ongoing support and problem solving for the team. Times for phone conferences can be established during the on-site sessions, but it is important for the coach to let team members know that they can call at other times if needed.

INTERAGENCY MEETINGS

If a number of programs have the same capacity-building consultant or are funded under the same or similar initiatives, a periodic gathering of team members from all the programs can help speed the capacity-building process. The coach can provide additional training on evaluation or other topics requested by the participants. Each meeting should be structured to allow participants to learn from each other and to establish supportive relationships with other participants. A format that includes time devoted to sharing successes, barriers, and lessons learned is enjoyable and beneficial for both the coach and evaluation team members. Time is also well spent asking each team to present a problem or barrier they are experiencing in their program or evaluation, followed by a facilitated problem-solving session with the entire group.

CONCLUSIONS

Community-based organizations and programs are now required to demonstrate effectiveness in order to receive and maintain funding. One way for programs or agencies to demonstrate their success is for staff members to conduct their own program evaluation. Some foundations and other funding entities assist community programs in building capacity for evaluation by providing specialized training and technical assistance as part of the funding process. Evaluation professionals who wish to work with family service agencies and other community-based organizations to build capacity for self-evaluation must be skilled not only at traditional program evaluation but also at adult learning, group facilitation, communication, and family services or other content areas.

In addition, evaluation professionals should either have skills in both quantitative and qualitative evaluation methods or be able to offer resources to support program staff in the use of mixed methods in their evaluation plans.

The approach to building capacity for program self-evaluation that is presented in this chapter reflects years of direct field experience with nonprofit organizations and other agencies that provide family services. Our approach includes assessing the organization's or program's readiness to learn and conduct program self-evaluation and combines initial training in basic program evaluation with ongoing on-site and distance technical assistance. Whenever possible, periodic interagency meetings are also held to provide peer support and to share successes and lessons learned.

There are a number of pitfalls related to building capacity for program self-evaluation that coaches may be able to avoid through careful planning and communication. As described in this chapter, many of these pitfalls or obstacles are related to issues of power, control, and leadership and to different expectations among stakeholders in the capacity-building process. We have presented the lessons we learned through our work in hopes that others will benefit from our experiences.

References

American Psychological Association. (2003). Guidelines on multicultural education, training, research, practice, and organizational change for psychologists. *American Psychologist, 58* (5), 377–402.

Andrews, A. B. (2004). Start at the end: empowerment evaluation product planning. *Evaluation and Program Planning, 27,* 275–85.

Andrews, A. B., Guadalupe, J. L., and Bolden, E. (2003). Faith, hope, and mutual support: Paths to empowerment as perceived by women in poverty. *Journal of Social Work Research and Evaluation, 4* (1), 5–18.

Andrews, A. B., Motes, P. S., Floyd, A. G., Flerx, V. C., and Lòpez-De Fede, A. (2005). Building evaluation capacity in community-based organizations: Reflections of an empowerment evaluation team. *Journal of Community Practice, 13* (4).

Brown, P. (1995). The role of the evaluator in comprehensive community initiatives. In J. P. Connell, A. C. Kubisch, L. B. Schorr, and C. H. Weiss (Eds.), *New approaches to evaluating community initiatives: Concepts, methods, and contexts* (Vol. 1, pp. 201–25). Queenstown, Md.: Aspen Institute.

Brown, L. D., and Tandon, R. (1983). Ideology and political economy in inquiry: Action research and participatory research. *Journal of Applied Behavioral Science, 19* (3), 277–94.

Brunner, I., and Guzman, A. (1989). Participatory evaluation: A tool to assess projects and empower people. In R. F. Conner and M. Hendricks (Eds.), *International innovations in evaluation methodology: New directions for program evaluation* (Vol. 42, pp. 9–19). San Francisco: Jossey-Bass.

Buros, O. (1989–present). Mental measurements yearbook. Highland Park, N.J.: Buros Institute.

Caldwell, B., and Bradley, R. (1984). *Home observation for measure of the environment (HOME)*. Little Rock: Center for Child Development and Education, College of Education, University of Arkansas.

Campobasso, L., and Davis D. (2001). *Progressive strategies.* Woodland Hills, Calif.: The California Wellness Foundation.

Denzin, N. (1978). *The research act* (2nd ed.). Englewood Cliffs, N.J.: Prentice Hall.

Denzin, N., and Lincoln, Y. (Eds.). (1994). Handbook of qualitative research. Thousand Oaks, Calif.: Sage.

Drisko, J. (1997). Strengthening qualitative studies and reports: Standards to promote academic integrity. *Journal of Social Work Education, 33*, 185–97.

Fetterman, D. M. (1989). *Ethnography: Step by step.* Newbury Park, Calif.: Sage.

Fetterman, D. M. (1994). Empowerment evaluation. *Evaluation Practice, 15* (1), 1–15.

Fetterman, D. M. (2001). Empowerment evaluation and self-determination: A practical approach toward program improvement and capacity building. In N. Schneiderman and M.A. Speers (Eds.), *Integrating behavioral and social sciences with public health* (pp. 321–50). Washington, D.C.: American Psychological Association.

Fetterman, D. M. (2003). Empowerment evaluation strikes a responsive cord. In S. I. Donaldson and M. Scriven (Eds.), *Evaluating social programs and problems: Visions for the new millenium.* The Claremont Symposium on Applied Social Psychology. Mahwah, N.J.: Lawrence Erlbaum.

Fetterman, D. M., Kaftarian, S., and Wandersman, A. (1996). *Empowerment evaluation: Knowledge and tools for self-assessment and accountability.* Thousand Oaks, Calif.: Sage.

Fetterman, D. M., and Wandersman, A. (2004). *Empowerment evaluation principles in practice.* New York: Guilford.

Fitz-Gibbon, C. T., and Morris, L. L. (1987). *How to design a program evaluation* (2nd ed.). New York: Sage.

Fitzpatrick, J. L., Sanders, J. R., and Worthen, B. R. (2003). *Program evaluation: Alternative approaches and practical guidelines* (3rd ed.). Boston: Allyn and Bacon.

Flerx, V. C. (1999). *Foundations of evaluation.* Columbia, S.C.: Institute for Families in Society, University of South Carolina.

Floyd, A., Andrews, A. B., Hess, P., Flerx, V. C., Rivers, J., Phillips, L., Whiting, J., Malson, M., and Kinnard, D. (2003). *Lessons learned and affirmed: The Duke Endowment Children and Families Program.* Columbia, S.C.: Institute for Families in Society, University of South Carolina.

Garvin, D. A. (1994, January). Building a learning organization. *Business Credit, 96* (1), 19–28.

Ginsberg, L. (2001). *Social work evaluation: Principles and methods.* Needham Heights, Mass.: Allyn and Bacon.

Glesne, C. (1999). *Becoming qualitative researchers* (2nd ed.). New York: Longman.

Grundy, S. (1986). Action research and human interests. In M. Emery and P. Long (Eds.), *Symposium, May 22–23, 1986, Research Network of the Australian Association of Adult Education.*

Guba, E., and Lincoln, Y. (1989). *Fourth generation evaluation.* Beverly Hills, Calif.: Sage.

Henggeler, S., and Shoenwald, S. (1994). Boot camps for juvenile offenders: Just say no. Journal of Child and Family Studies, 3, 243–248.

Hernandez, G., and Visher, M. G. (2001) *Creating a culture of inquiry: Changing methods—and minds—on the use of evaluation in nonprofit organizations.* San Francisco: James Irving Foundation.

Hess, P., and Flerx, V. C. (2003). Findings from the IFS consultants/coaches evaluation survey. In Floyd, A., Andrews, A. B., Hess, P., Flerx, V. C., Rivers, J., Phillips, L., Whiting, J., Malson, M., and Kinnard, D. *Lessons learned and affirmed: The Duke Endowment Children and Families Program.* Columbia, S.C.: Institute for Families in Society, University of South Carolina.

Hess, P., McGowan, B., and Botsko, M. (2003). *Nurturing the one, supporting the many: The Center for Family Life in Sunset Park, Brooklyn.* New York: Columbia University Press.

Impara, J., and Plake, B. (Eds.). (1998). *The thirteenth mental measurements yearbook.* Lincoln, Neb: Buros Institute of Mental Measurements.

Israel, B. A., Checkoway, B., Schulz, A., and Zimmerman, M. (1994). Health education and community empowerment: Conceptualizing and measuring perceptions of individual, organizational, and community control. *Health Education Quarterly, 21* (2), 149–70.

Joint Committee on Standards for Educational Evaluation. (1994). *The program evaluation standards.* Thousand Oaks, Calif.: Sage.

Jones, R. (Ed.). (1996). *Handbook of tests and measurements for black populations* (Vols. 1 and 2). Hampton, Va,: Cobb and Henry.

Kemmis, S., and McTaggart, R. (1988) *The action research planner* (3rd ed.). Geelong, Victoria, Australia: Deakin University.

Kirby, D. (1997). *No easy answers: Research findings on programs to reduce teen pregnancy.* Washington, D.C.: National Campaign to Prevent Teen Pregnancy Task Force on Effective Programs and Research.

Kirby, D. (2001). Understanding what works and what doesn't in reducing adolescent sexual risk taking. *Family Planning Perspectives, 33* (6), 276–81.

Kirby, D., Barth, R. P., Leland, N., and Fetro, J. V. (1991). Reducing the risk: Impact of new curriculum on sexual risk-taking. *Family Planning Perspectives, 23* (6), 253–63.

Krippendorff, K. (1980). *Content analysis. An introduction to its methodology.* Beverly Hills, Calif.: Sage.

Lagana, L., and Hayes, D. (1993). Contraceptive health programs for adolescents: A critical review. *Adolescence, 28* (110), 347–59.

Law Enforcement News. (1996). When it comes to the young, anti-drug efforts are going to pot. *Law Enforcement News, 22,* 441–47.

Linney, J. A., and Wandersman, A. (1991). *Prevention Plus III: Assessing alcohol and other drug prevention programs at the school and community level: A four-step guide to useful program assessment.* Rockville, Md.: U.S. Department of Health and Human Services.

Mertens, D. M. (1999). Inclusive evaluation: Implications of transformative theory for evaluation. *American Journal of Evaluation, 20,* 1–14.

Miller, B., and Card, J. J. (Eds.). (1992). Preventing adolescent pregnancy: Model programs and evaluations. Sage Focus Editions (Vol. 140, pp. 1–27). Thousand Oaks, Calif.: Sage.

Morgan, D. (Ed.). (1993). *Successful focus groups.* Newbury Park, Calif.: Sage.

Nyden, P., and Wiewel, W. (1992). Collaborative research: Harnessing the tensions between researcher and practitioner. *The American Sociologist, 23,* 43–55.

Patton, M. (1990). *Qualitative evaluation and research methods* (2nd ed.). Newbury Park, Calif.: Sage.

Rosenberg, M. (1965). *Society and the adolescent self-image.* Princeton, N.J.: Princeton University Press.

Sabo, K. (2004). Exploring the relationships between evaluation capacity, evaluative thinking, and organizational effectiveness. Presentation at Evaluation 2004, eighteenth annual conference of the American Evaluation Association (November 3–6), Atlanta.

Sarri, R., and Sarri, C. (1992). Organizational and community change through participatory action research. *Administration in Social Work, 16,* 99–122.

SenGupta, S., Hopson, R., and Thompson-Robison, M. (2004). Cultural competence in evaluation: An overview. In M. Thompson-Robinson, R. Hopson, and S. SenGupta (Eds.) *In search of cultural competence in evaluation: Toward principles and practices* (pp. 5–19), San Francisco: Jossey-Bass, Wiley Periodicals.

Spradley, J. (1980). *Participant observation.* Fort Worth, Tex.: Harcourt College.

Stake, R. (1995). *The art of case study research.* Thousand Oaks, Calif.: Sage.

Stevenson, J. F., Mitchell, R. E., and Florin, P. (1996). Evaluation and self-direction in community prevention coalitions. In D. Fetterman, S. Kafterian, and A. Wandersman (Eds.). *Empowerment evaluation: Knowledge and tools for self-assessment and accountability* (pp. 201–33). Thousand Oaks, Calif.: Sage.

Symonette, H. (2004). Walking pathways toward becoming a culturally competent evaluator: Boundaries, borderlands, and border crossings. In M. Thompson-Robinson, R. Hopson, and S. SenGupta (Eds.) *In search of cultural competence in evaluation: Toward principles and practices* (pp. 95–109), San Francisco: Jossey-Bass, Wiley Periodicals.

Thomas, V. (2004). Building a contextually responsive evaluation framework: Lessons from working with urban school interventions. *New Directions for Evaluation, 101,* 3–23.

United Way of America. (1996). *Measuring program outcomes: a practical approach.* Alexandria, Va: Author.

Weiss, H., and Jacobs, F. (1988). *Evaluating family programs.* New York: Aldine De Gruyter.

Wholey, J. S., Hatry, H. P., and Newcomer, K. E. (1994). *Handbook of practical program evaluation.* New York: Jossey-Bass.

Whyte, W. F., Greenwood, D. J., and Lazes, P. (1991). Participatory action research: Through practice to science in social research. In W. F. Whyte (Ed.), *Participatory action research* (pp. 19–56). Newbury Park, Calif.: Sage.

Conclusion

Consultants who contribute to the building of capacity in organizations and communities are provided a myriad of opportunities not only to enhance the professional and lay service efforts and outcomes of these organization and communities but also to indirectly support the families and children that they serve. However, as described by the contributors to this volume, consultants must be prepared in order to meet these opportunities successfully.

Several themes are woven throughout this volume with regard to successful organizational and community capacity building. These include clarity regarding expectation and role; individualization of the goals and processes of each effort; understanding and ability to address the complexity of each capacity-building effort; achieving a balance between the ideal and the real; maintaining ethical practice in the midst of politics and divergent agendas; and recognition of the demands associated with the process of coaching. Each of these will be reviewed here as they have been highlighted in each chapter.

CLARITY

The effectiveness of the consultant in his or her possibly multiple roles depends upon the clarity of all parties regarding expectations and tasks. Consultants must clarify with those seeking their assistance whether what they are being asked to provide is *consultation*—giving expert or professional advice; *technical assistance*—giving concrete and tangible help or support for a specific purpose, such as modeling or training; or *service*—functioning as if the consultant were an agency employee in a delimited area of responsibility, such as writing grants or constructing databases. As stressed in chapter 2 and depicted in table 2.1, these roles are related, but the activities undertaken in each differ. Assuring that clarity regarding expectations and tasks is achieved is the responsibility of the consultant and is a necessary prerequisite to productive relationships and ultimately to effectiveness.

INDIVIDUALIZATION

Capacity-building efforts occur within a wide range of organizations and communities and focus upon one or more goals and processes specific to an organization's or community's situation. Therefore, the goals and processes of various capacity-building efforts are necessarily individualized. One size does not fit all. In order to tailor the service provided to specific organizational and community needs, capacity-building consultants must have highly developed assessment skills as well as an excellent understanding of what is required for effective collaboration, technical assistance, strategic planning, and program self-evaluation.

COMPLEXITY

As illustrated by the examples throughout this volume, capacity-building efforts are rarely simple. Rather, such efforts can invariably be characterized as complex due to the competing interests and perceptions of multiple and diverse stakeholders, such as funders, program participants and consumers, program staff, and community leaders; the economic, cultural, and political contexts; and the resulting varied definitions of needs and goals. The coach enters this complex social situation bringing his or her own expertise and perspective. Remaining ever mindful of, seeking to understand, and taking into account the multiple factors relevant to planning and implementing, capacity-building efforts are essential ongoing responsibilities of the coach.

BALANCE

Yet another theme in this volume is the tension between the ideal and the real. An effective capacity-building consultant will be able to identify and balance these tensions. Such tensions include, for example, those between "good practice," (i.e., evidence-based, theoretically defensible programming), and the local reality, including resources available, practitioners' knowledge and skills, and political forces. Tensions may similarly exist between the goals of an effort and the limited time frame within which progress must be made or between the desire for effective collaboration and the historically isolationist stance of community agencies. Capacity-building consultants must provide information concerning best practices while assessing with stakeholders the degree to which best practices can be achieved in an individual situation.

ETHICS

Professionals who enter into relationships with staff members at all levels of community organizations and with stakeholders whose interests are often competing for the purpose of enhancing the capacities of those with whom they work must adhere to ethical standards of practice. Ethical challenges inevitably arise as one practices in arenas where the stakes are high. Continued program funding may rely on a glowing program evaluation; stakeholders' personal needs and agendas may conflict, resulting in interpersonally or politically charged interactions; or a coach may enter a situation with one understanding only to discover that the expertise needed is not the expertise the coach has brought to the table. Also, organizations may not be ready to undertake the process they have retained the coach to assist them with. Confidentiality, appropriate boundaries in collegial relationships, and refusing to take on work for which one is not qualified are only a few of the areas in which consultants must be watchful with regard to maintaining both professional and personal ethics.

DEMANDING BUT WORTHWHILE

The process of coaching organizations and assisting community capacity-building efforts is demanding of time and of energy. Coaches must recognize these inevitable costs and plan accordingly. As indicated in great detail in chapters 4 through 6, using a team approach to coaching not only provides deeper and broader experience than can any one coach alone, it also assures support for each of the coaches on the team.

When roles and expectations are clear, services are individualized and take into account best practices, local realities, and professional ethics. Thus, inevitable complexities are anticipated and addressed, and efforts to build organizational and community capacity as described in this volume can make an important difference to those who serve children and families. As a community's professional and lay service providers are empowered with expanded knowledge and skills, their ongoing service within their communities ultimately creates a stronger society for one and all.

Sample Generic Outline for Final Evaluation Report

■ ■ ■

Name of Organization

Name of Project/Program

EVALUATION REPORT

Dates of period covered in evaluation report

PROGRAM SYNOPSIS

Description: Use this section to describe your program/project. Include a statement indicating sources of support for your project. Identify any organizational partners involved in the project.
Planned and actual cost of the program.

PLANNED ACTIVITIES AND OUTCOMES

Goals: Describe the primary goals of your project. What specific changes are you trying to accomplish? For whom (target groups)? Where?

Objectives: List measurable activity objectives. List measurable outcome objectives. Refer to the inputs, outputs, and outcomes listed in your logic model.

Program Activities (Actual Performance)

Include a statement indicating when your program actually began and a general description of the efforts of your program.

INPUTS

Program resources: What resources have made this program possible? In what ways were contributions made to your program? Staff (numbers/hours/roles)? Volunteers (numbers/hours/roles)? Office space? Funds expended during this reporting period? Other relevant resources?

Program participants: What did participants bring to the program? How did they become connected?

Intake: Was a recruitment process used? Was a referral process used? Describe your recruitment/referral process in detail (number of referrals or recruitment efforts; sources of referral, recruitment; number of intakes or contacts for program involvement; number of persons starting in your program, etc.).

Intervention: Describe *general demographic characteristics* of persons involved in your program: How many people have been served for any period of time during the reporting period? What is the percentage of those served relative to those recruited or referred? Describe persons served, e.g., by age; gender; marital status; race/ethnicity; geographical location; educational level; income level; or other relevant characteristics. If possible, use tables or charts; report in raw numbers and percentages.

OUTPUTS

What products have resulted from your program activities?

Program participants: Number (percentage) who *completed* program during the reporting period; average amount of service per participant; dropout rate (those who terminated before planned completion).

Number/kind of activities (e.g. groups, training, workshops, sessions, home visits, other relevant units of service) provided.

Time spent in program (average hours for each activity provided; average time attended by participants).

Satisfaction with program services: Based on survey or other data, indicate degree of satisfaction expressed by consumers/participants? Volunteers? Staff? Partners? Referral sources? Other stakeholders?

Other outputs: Include products/efforts of your agency, community, volunteers, partners/ collaborators (e.g. training manuals, brochures, other),

EFFICIENCY

How efficient is the program, given outputs relative to inputs? Is the program reaching the intended population?

Program Outcomes

Describe the changes that have occurred with your program participants as a result of your program. Describe any other changes that have occurred because of your program. How has it affected your agency? Community? Volunteers? Partners/collaborators?

Results: Use narration and other appropriate structures to summarize data/results gathered about your outcomes. The results summarized should initially address those outlined in your logic model. Describe the data sources, collection plans, and evaluation strategies that led to the results. If you have used pre/post comparisons or intervention/control-group data, describe basic procedures. Once you have addressed the primary outcomes as listed in your logic model, address any additional outcomes that have occurred because of your program.

Conclusions: Use narrative discussion to bring meaning to the data discussed in the "Results" section.

Program Quality

Beyond the performance and outcome numbers, what else do you know about your program's efforts?

Fidelity: If your program is based on a particular model, how has fidelity to the model been assured? How does the actual program differ from the model?

Quality standards: How does the program compare with the standards of quality that you have chosen for the program?

Voice of the consumer: Offer vignettes about participant/consumer successes and barriers and quotes from participants/consumers about the program. If possible, include pictures (with participant permission, preferably in black and white for reproduction).

Lessons learned: Include a discussion that

- describes the impressions of staff, board members, volunteers, and participants about strengths and vulnerabilities of program and how they have been/can be managed;
- tells the program story, especially what has been learned about how best to help your target population and how the program has been changed to better meet these needs;
- deals frankly with any delays or mistakes; describe what was learned from them and steps taken to address these problems or plans for addressing these problems;
- describes and positive or negative unintended effects.

Conclusions and Future Plans

Evaluation summary: Overall, what is the value of this program? What are the benefits relative to the investments?

Next steps: Briefly summarize your current efforts and your plans for the future of your program.

Endnotes (If appropriate, include endnotes similar to the following in the report):

This report is based on data routinely collected from participants. The data were reviewed on a regular basis by an evaluation team composed of the following: (*list names, titles, and roles*, e.g., staff, board, interagency representatives, consumers, etc). The team reviewed program information; discussed lessons learned; and made recommendations for program improvements.

(Name of Program) is committed to continuous learning. Anyone wishing to share comments about this report is invited to contact (name, address, phone).

Index